DATE DUE

JAMES, JOYCE, AND OTHERS

James, Joyce, and Others

By

A. J. A. WALDOCK

Professor of English Literature in the University of Sydney

Essay Index Reprint Series

Originally published by:

WILLIAMS & NORGATE LTD.

BOOKS FOR LIBRARIES PRESS, INC.
FREEPORT, NEW YORK

First published 1937
Reprinted 1967

PRINTED IN THE UNITED STATES OF AMERICA

CONTENTS

JAMES, JOYCE, AND OTHERS

HENRY JAMES

IF one reads (as one may, in old numbers of *The Atlantic Monthly* and other magazines) the earliest reviews that Henry James wrote, one sees that before he had reached his middle twenties he had formed some notion of what the ideal novel should be. To make this notion quite clear to himself, to realise all its implications and express them in his own work, was, speaking quite literally, the occupation and the joy of his lifetime. He just succeeded within his lifetime—which was a long one—in accomplishing his purpose. His last three completed novels, the novels of his elderly years—*The Wings of the Dove*, *The Ambassadors* and *The Golden Bowl*—are the final embodiment of that idea of the novel with which, so many years before, he began ; and his progress, throughout all that time, was towards these three great books. There were lapses, naturally, but the line was always upward and upward. The last three finished novels are not quite the latest work we have from him. He left two fragments, *The Ivory Tower* and *The Sense of the Past*. The war broke into both these books, broke into him, indeed, and left him for a while almost sapped of his " sacred rage," so that what at another time would have absorbed all his zest seemed in some of these dark moments a mere playing with " fiddlesticks." It is clear, however, that neither of the two unfinished novels would have shown any further important advances in technique ; we may regret their incompleteness, for all that. *The Sense of the Past*, in particular, would have been one of the most charming of all his excursions into the phantasmal world ; in the theme of this book James seemed to find a certain relief from the numbing pressure of events, and could plunge himself into the writing of it with some of the old exhilaration.

But, technically, he had, no doubt, reached his goal. He could go no farther, and, as it was, had already gone too far for the majority of his readers, who for some time past had found their powers of endurance increasingly taxed. James watched them, as one by one they fell off, with a humorous sadness—" ruefulness " is his word—until even the elect began to fail him. It was, indeed, an unrelenting progress, and drastic in more than one way. When the time came for the preparation of the massive New York edition of 1908, the earlier work was treated ruthlessly. Some delightful novels —even *The Bostonians*, even *Washington Square*—were excluded, at least temporarily, from the canon ; others, such as *The American* and *Roderick Hudson*, were mercilessly revised. Edmund Gosse was but one sensitive critic who protested at the treatment which old favourites were seen to be receiving ; when it was clear that even delicate stories like *Daisy*

2

Miller were not to be spared, some degree of horror came to be mingled with the protests. And James, for his part, was hurt by such objections—even a little resentful of them ; for to him there was no question of what was right, and the obtuseness of his friends made him suffer.

These revisions (to pause on them for a moment) are very interesting, admitting one as they do to a sight of Henry James at work. Their effect is by no means limited to a superficial re-touching of the style, though it is often suggested that the aim was no more than that. " Mr. Newman," remarked E. F. Hale, " seems an American gentleman who in the Seventies had had the advantage of reading Mr. James's later writing." Once he held that " love made a fool of a man " ; now that condition is, for him, " too consistent with asininity." But really the alterations go quite beyond " style " in the restricted sense, and amount to nothing less than an effort to impose the later technique on the earlier material. To James's mature eye a novel like *The American* seemed only half-written : as if the book behind or underneath the printed words had never yet been brought into full existence. He tells us of his experiences in re-reading the early novels ; in some cases the task of revision seemed patently impossible and he did not attempt it ; in others, and in varying degrees in each, it was a question of going over the writing inch by inch until, as far as could be, the true life of the book was made actual and visible. Only patient comparison can reveal the magnitude of such an undertaking and show the many results he was trying to achieve. The method of narration is itself altered, so that in *The American*, for instance, by countless minute changes of phrasing, the whole story is pressed back more fully into the mind of the hero Newman : it is through his " delegated sensibility " that we are to receive our report, and the author's own " guarantee," so frequently offered in the original, is now ruthlessly torn up. In short, James does what he can to re-write *The American* in the manner of *The Ambassadors*. It was a task that could not be completely achieved, but he would have considered it a betrayal of his artistic faith not to make the attempt. He tries, thus, to improve the structure by importing innumerable phrases of the form " as he would have said," " as he might have called it," " as he named it to himself." Such details are not trivial, for their cumulative effect is to move the account one degree back. Everywhere the assertion of the author is avoided, or at least softened, and his intrusiveness checked : a mere statement of a fact becomes a report of an impression of Newman's. " He flattered himself that he was not in love, but his biographer may be supposed to know better " : this was " sorry business " to the later James, and all clumsiness of the sort had to be reshaped or replaced. It is like a great feat of engineering : a huge fabric from top to bottom must be overhauled, the strains and stresses examined and redistributed, every weakness buttressed, every unsoundness corrected. So, for another example out of dozens of the kind, we had been told of Newman and of Madame de

4

Cintré that "whether or no he did occasionally bore her, it is probable that on the whole she liked him only the better for his absence of embarrassed scruples." In the revised version we are told nothing so directly : it is recorded, instead, that "he seemed at least to know that even if she actually suffered she liked him better, on the whole, with too few fears than with too many." The narrator's self-denying ordinance is exhibited clearly here : he will not, he must not—indeed, in accordance with his self-imposed law he cannot—tell us what Madame de Cintré liked or did not like ; all he can legitimately tell us is what Newman imagined she liked, or what he seemed to think she felt. To "stick to the logical centre"—it is now the rule of rules.

But all the changes, whatever their nature in detail, are informed by one principle, lead to one end ; it is the search for full truth of statement that controls them ; James is engaged in intensifying the expression of a theme previously, but not to his mature judgment "entirely," expressed. He had become, for one thing, wiser in the interval and his deepened understanding—the edge his perceptions had taken from all the "wear and tear of discrimination"—shows in many a substitution. "It is a proof of cleverness," Newman had said, "to be happy without doing anything." Of cleverness only ? In the new version the word is changed : it becomes "power." In the old text Newman and Madame de Cintré are talking of the detestation in which he, the American, is held by her family :

5

" I don't strike myself as a man to hate," he says. Madame de Cintré replies : " I suppose that a man who may be liked may also be disliked." It is a commonplace remark. Compare the precision of the new rendering, which offers a new meaning, or says for the first time what was meant : " ' I suppose a man who may inspire strong feelings,' she thoughtfully opined, ' must take his chance of what they are '." The speakers have become, in truth, more thoughtful—more capable, too, of defining what they think.

They have become, also, more visible. Often, in the dialogue, a bare record will be enriched with notations of look and demeanour, so that, where before we listened merely, now we both watch and listen :

Old version : " ' Yes, she is very beautiful,' said Newman."

New version : " ' Yes, she is very beautiful,' said Newman, while he covered Claire with his bright still protection."

We read his eyes as he speaks. Again :

Old version : " ' No, they don't,' she said."

New version : " ' Scarcely,' she said, with the gentlest, oddest distinctness."

The meaning is augmented and sharpened here, for the context makes plain the point of that evasive annotation. Sometimes the words of the dialogue are abandoned and, for more significance, replaced by a description of gesture and look :

Old version : " ' That's a poor reason,' said Madame de Cintré, smiling."

6

New version : " She gave, still with her charming eyes on him, the slowest, gentlest headshake."

Imagery, too, is much more fully used than before, and again, the effect (though occasionally at some loss of ease and simplicity) is of enrichment. In the original *American* Newman listens to Madame de Cintré as she talks affectionately of her brother— " listened sometimes with a certain harmless jealousy ; he would have liked to divert some of her tender allusions to his own credit." The figure, if figure there be, conveys little ; but observe the precision and fullness of the new rendering : " Newman listened sometimes with a vague irrepressible pang ; if he could only have caught in his own cup a few drops of that overflow ! " These are the touches—and they are innumerable—that lift *The American* into completer existence.

Daisy Miller was a different matter. The added commentary can often, it is true, illumine and intensify here as it did in *The American*. The portraiture, for instance, of Mrs. Miller—Daisy's dreamily remote mother—is completed by the changes. But the possibilities of enriching the substance of this story were fewer, and the dangers of injury to the exquisite light grace of the original expression much greater. James's taste had altered in many little ways : he had come, for example, to dislike intensely the " said's " and " replied's " of dialogue and makes it now a point of honour to avoid them : and even changes of this kind seem a heaviness on the story of *Daisy Miller*. " When she heard Winterbourne's voice she quickly turned her head. ' Well, I declare ! ' she said. ' I told you I should come, you know,' Winterbourne rejoined, smiling." Such straightforwardness made the mature Henry James wince. Elaborately he circumvents these commonplace formulæ : " Daisy was engaged in some pretty babble with her hostess, but when she heard Winterbourne's voice she quickly turned her head with a ' Well, I declare ! ' which he met smiling. ' I told you I should come, you know '." And there are many places—apart from details of this kind—where one feels that a freshness has been spoilt by the attempt at a fuller rendering, a naturalness sacrificed without a compensating gain. Winterbourne asks Daisy, ceremoniously, to row with him on the lake : " She only stood there laughing." It is enough to give us the picture : we know, with what has gone before, exactly why she laughs. The new version spoils the simplicity : " She only remained an elegant image of free light irony."

The story is a little disfigured, too, by quite a different type of change. James came to feel that he must secure colloquial fidelity and make his Americans speak in appropriate dialect : he does it by sprinkling " ain't's " and " guesses " through their talk. We feel, even in *The American,* that such alterations accomplish very little and were a pity, but in *Daisy Miller* they seem a real blemish. Before, young Randolph was content to say of his sister, " She's an American girl " ; now he adds, " You bet." Before, he said " to Italy," " to America " ; now he says " t'Italy," " t'America." Before, he

8

said " I am going to the Pincio " ; now he says " I
am going to go it on the Pincio." Randolph is an
amusing and irresponsible urchin, and it is not
perhaps of much account to us just how his " harsh
little voice " framed its syllables ; but we wish that
the dainty lips of his sister had continued to say
" isn't " and not " ain't."

But all such changes, for better or worse, came
later. It is interesting to turn back for a little to
the earlier manner—or, for a really sensational
contrast, to the earliest. One may find in *The
Atlantic Monthly* for March, 1865, a small piece of
fiction from the pen of the very young Henry James.
It is called *The Story of a Year*, and might quite as
easily have made its appearance in *The Quiver*. It
is a sentimental romance of the days of Civil War :
of a girl and her soldier-lover and her change of
heart in his absence, and of the happy ending
despite the sadness ; but the interest is in the
method of it. It abounds in apostrophes—" Alas,
Elizabeth, that you had no mother !"—in moralis-
ings, and every kind of free intrusion on the part
of the author. He will intersperse some general
reflections and then take his reader confidentially
by the arm.: " Good reader, this narrative is averse
to retrospect . . . " The story makes one laugh, as
quaint old unrecognisable photographs of a person
one knows very well make one laugh ; rub one's
eyes as one will, it is impossible to catch the faintest
resemblance, to discover even a sign that might
identify the author of this story with Henry James.
And the same is true—or nearly true—of everything

he published within the next few years ; there were many short stories for the magazines, hardly any of them reprinted.

Ten years and more went by before he was ready to write a full-length novel. Then, with *Roderick Hudson*, he began a series that went on for a dozen years or so ; through all this period his method was developing, but not altering greatly. He advanced from *The American* to *The Portrait of a Lady*, and from that again to *The Tragic Muse*. In *The Tragic Muse* (1890) faint indications may be observed, especially in the management of the conversations, of an approaching change of some magnitude : little ruffles appear on the style suggesting a breeze from a new direction. The theatre still attracted him and it was in these years that he made his most valiant efforts to write a successful drama ; but the time for that had long since passed. The developed mannerism, if there had been no other disabilities, disqualified him positively from now on for theatrical work. His dialogue—the vague hintings, the obscure circlings—had become impossible for practical use on the stage : a glance at almost any page of almost any of the later plays will prove that. He returned then from such disappointments to his main occupation, and in *The Spoils of Poynton* his final method is well in evidence. He was now clearly committed to it. In the last years of the century he wrote *The Awkward Age*, one of the most difficult of all the novels. Then in 1902 came *The Wings of the Dove ;* after that, in successive years, *The Ambassadors* and *The Golden Bowl*.

Let us dwell for a little, however, on the middle years, say 1876 to 1890, the period that begins with *Roderick Hudson* and ends with *The Tragic Muse*. Here, no doubt, will always be found James's most popular books. They are in the main straightforward, and, apart from the relief their clarity affords, possess many attractions. The best of them —and none can be placed higher than *The Portrait of a Lady*—have a suave and genial loveliness, curious to compare with the more difficult beauty of the later books, and especially of the last three. The gulf between the two styles is really amazing ; in the final period James is more intensely, more sombrely, preoccupied—has settled thoroughly to the business of his art, which has at the same time some of the marks of a religion. In the earlier phase the earnestness, though it is there, is not so profound, and the reader benefits by the lighter demands on him. The manner itself is very different—lucid, pointed, fresh, with a crisp tingle to it. In these earlier books the stream runs sparkling and limpid, though it has deeps ; later we feel ourselves carried on slow-moving fathomless rivers, full of strange eddies and involved swirls. The earlier style is not distinguished by image—which became James's chief resource in expression, indeed the only technique adequate to the infinite refinements of his meaning—but rather by a certain tang in the language that may amount at times to epigram. Chapters are often made to end with a little sharp snap—almost an audible click—of surprise or irony or paradox, some tart rejoinder by a character, some spirited comment from the author, so that certain of the conclusions remind one of the laugh upon which a curtain falls. James's taste altered in this regard, and it is very curious to notice how often, in the course of his revisions, he will seem to go out of his way to burr the point of an over-sharp phrase, and will take the neatness out of quite a mild antithesis. Winterbourne (of *Daisy Miller*), musing at night amid the ruins " remembered that if nocturnal meditations in the Colosseum are recommended by the poets they are deprecated by the doctors." Even the harmless sting of that playful remark was extracted : Winterbourne, in the later text, rather heavily " remembered that if nocturnal meditation thereabouts was the fruit of a rich literary culture it was none the less deprecated by medical science." Nevertheless much of the original flavour remains even in the revised texts. The effects are not readily detachable, depending as they do on dozens of associations that only the whole novel can supply. But we have many whimsical exactitudes of this kind : the heroine of *The Bostonians*, faintly amused by a thought, makes " a vague sound in her throat —a sort of pensive, private reference to the idea of laughter." Mrs. Farrinder, in the same novel, is a leader of feminists with an imposing presence suggestive of the public-platforms on which she spends so much of her life : she " at almost any time had the air of being introduced by a few remarks." Often there will be an ironic sparkle : the heroine of *Washington Square* is " affectionate, docile, obedient and much addicted to speaking the

truth " ; Mr. Goodwood, in *The Portrait of a Lady*,
" speaks a good deal, but he doesn't talk." This
kind of vivacity is quite foreign to the later James.
The heroine of *The Portrait of a Lady* is " mistress of
a wedge of brown-stone violently driven into Fifty-
Third Street." Sometimes, again, a pungency will
sharpen a more serious perception : " There's
nothing makes us feel so much alive as to see others
die. That's the sensation of life—the sense that we
remain."

And in these earlier books there are other relaxa-
tions : diversions of various kinds, little scraps of
recorded observation that give pleasure by the way.
We need expect no such relief in the later novels ;
there the rigour closes down. But here James will
introduce many a note, of comment or description,
that refreshes the mind and remains agreeably in
the memory : like the account of the little American
boy, brought up in a French school, whose native
speech became so strongly influenced by the French
idiom of his playmates that he would talk of
being " defended " to go near the water, and of
the necessity of " obeying to " his nurse : a veritable
trifle, yet a trifle that gives the mind a moment's
holiday. No novel is so full of such refreshment as
The Portrait of a Lady : that was partly deliberate
(James did nothing unconsciously) for he suspected
a possible " thinness " in the theme, and to " supply"
it brought in the " group of attendants and enter-
tainers " and " little touches and inventions and
enhancements " besides, for our amusement. The
result shows what he could do in such ways when he

13   B 2

wished—in light caricature, and satiric or pathetic or humorous delineation ; no novel of his is so rich in interest.

But, of course, as he would have demurred, that word " interest " begs the whole question. The " liveliness " that marks *The Portrait of a Lady* was, in a sense, a concession, and as time went on he felt himself less and less inclined to make concessions ; his own interest was too strongly held elsewhere.

Henry James's latest manner has two main distinguishing features : there is the idiosyncrasy of style, and there is the new method.

As for the style, it became almost a dialect ; so much so that on rare occasions the effect may even be a little like that of a hoax. His expression became so specialised for subtleties that he was as if compelled to express any idea subtly : it is possible, at moments, to demonstrate that the complication is purely in the expression. But that is exceptional. In general, it was an instrument wonderfully perfected for his needs. It is difficult to isolate its special character or to find for it, in any one image, a suitable likeness. At moments the mind is recalled, unwillingly, to Mr. H. G. Wells's irresistible picture of Henry James " clambering over huge metaphors " ; the description possesses at least the truth of caricature ; and yet how rarely do these late metaphors fail to justify themselves. I may quote one further instance from the revised *American*. Newman, at Madame de Cintré's receptions, has a habit of listening and of saying little ; he is not bored, neither is he absent-minded : but the precise quality of these " silent sessions " of his remains, in the original text, a little vague. The truth is that James's resources in expression were not at the time quite equal to conveying the subtlety. There is only one way in which it can be conveyed—by an image, and an elaborate image at that. We see, then, how the later James comes to the rescue : " The Marquise Urbain had once found occasion to declare to him that he reminded her, in company, of a swimming-master she had once had who would never himself go into the water and who yet, at the baths, *en costume de ville,* managed to control and direct the floundering scene without so much as getting splashed. He had so made her angry, she professed, when he turned her awkwardness to ridicule. Newman affected her in like manner as keeping much too dry : it was urgent for her that *he* should be splashed—otherwise what was he doing at the baths ?—and she even hoped to get him into the water."

But perhaps the most lasting impression that the style leaves in the mind is that of a certain regenerating power : it seems to possess a principle of life by which it expands and grows and sprouts and buds : before our eyes, an idea comes into being, develops, divides itself, multiplies. Here, for a second example, is a passage from the very late autobiographical volume, *The Middle Years ;* James is speaking of the notion of the " end of one's youth," and of what meaning the phrase may contain :

" We are never old, that is, we never cease easily

to be young, for *all* life at the same time : youth is an army, the whole battalion of our faculties and our freshness, our passion and our illusions, on a considerably reluctant march into the enemy's country, the country of the general lost freshness ; and I think it throws out at least as many stragglers behind as skirmishers ahead—stragglers who often catch up but belatedly with the main body, and even in many a case never catch up at all. Or under another figure it is a book in several volumes, and even at this a mere instalment of a large library of life, with a volume here and there closing, as something in the clap of its covers may assure us, while another remains either completely agape or kept open by a fond finger thrust in between the leaves."

It was, as well, a perfectly natural style, in the sense of being quite spontaneous and personal. He used, as his friends tell, to converse in much the same way, so that to listen to his casual talk was often to have the sensation of " being present at the actual construction of a little palace of thought." The description is A. C. Benson's, who adds that voice and gesture would make plain what on a page might have been tough and coagulated. Then there were the favourite expressions. Certain words in James could almost be used as a test of period, were other evidence wanting : one is " bristle," another is " portentous." *The Portrait of a Lady* can hardly furnish more than a stray example of each : but count them in *The Golden Bowl* or in any later preface ! One other element of vocabulary is curious. To the very end, and even when he is writing in his manner of extreme elaborateness, he likes to bring in a colloquialism. He declines as a rule to assume responsibility for it : he will handle it daintily between inverted commas, or else transfer his guilt to a character (" She would be hanged— she conversed with herself in strong language— if . . . "), but he will relish it nevertheless. It is a liking that accords with his fancy for imagery of the homeliest kind : he will turn very ordinary things to metaphor in the most luxurious fashion. But, of course, the truth is that his style was, in an essential way, colloquial ; it was the style of his novels, his letters (" a friendly bulletin would produce a document like a great tapestry ") and his speech ; not his native utterance, but the utterance that had become, by acquirement, his one natural, and indeed his only possible, mode of expression. We know, too, that his latest novels were actually talked—to his secretary.

But they were not only talked, they were talked over : talked over aloud while his secretary—this was before the final dictation—took down all that he said. We have in printed form the record of two such preliminary discussions : they concern the unfinished novels, *The Ivory Tower* and *The Sense of the Past ;* it was his custom, when a novel was finished, to destroy these notes. Analogous documents must exist, but I doubt whether a novelist has ever given a more fascinating glimpse of himself at work than James in these survivals. They are not first drafts, they are informal self-communings. That is their special interest and the quality that makes them even more revealing than the prefaces. The prefaces, after the event, retrace the procedure, but these notes—James called them " rough scenarios "—show a novel in the living processes of creation ; the pains, the joys, the anxieties, the hesitations, the seekings, the findings are there for us, as James thinks aloud ; for that is precisely what in these notes he does. The full interest is only to be gained, naturally, by a comparison of the notes with what was completed of the work ; but even in themselves they give a sense of the adventure that writing was for him. It was adventure all the time —" high amusement "—and actually the record takes on the form at times of a little drama. We listen to him, for example, as he walks up and down in the study at Lamb House, pondering *The Sense of the Past*. There is some little difficulty with the plot, a special connection he wants, a " clou d'argent " that at first will not come to his hand ; so he puts the matter aside for a moment with a reminder to himself, " Find it, find it." Presently he returns to it : " It must consist of something he [the hero] has to do, some condition he has to execute, some moment he has to traverse, or rite or sacrifice he has to perform, say even some liability he has to face." Then, as he murmurs to himself the word liability, he feels himself " warmer " : he is coming nearer to what he requires. " I seem to see it " (his voice must have rendered these excitements), " it glimmers upon me. When I call it a liability I seem to catch it by the tip of the tail." But for a while it was still elusive. " Let me figure it out a bit," he goes on,

" and under gentle, or rather patiently firm, direct pressure, it will come out." So, presently, it does, and we have an exclamation of triumph, " That's it, that's it." [1]

All the ups and downs, all the varying fortunes, are recorded, for the talk, as will be seen, is absolutely to himself (his secretary merely overhearing) and therefore utterly informal. There is no attempt at " style," though it is amusing to observe how the idiom comes through nevertheless, often heightening and caricaturing itself in vast convolutions and heapings up of adjective and adverb,[2] as James experiments with one word after another to see what stimulus for his imagination may lurk in it. Nor is the experience merely intellectual : James in these moments is *living* very fully and his emotions are deeply engaged. " Oh," he will burst out, " I see somehow such beautiful things that I can hardly keep step with myself to expatiate and adumbrate coherently enough." But it is not all triumph. He has worries, doubts—an occasional sharp fright. In the midst of his elation he will suddenly be pulled up by the thought of something wrong—a difficulty

[1] The idea, as James worked it out, was this : the man of *The Sense of the Past* becomes aware, in certain circumstances, of his counterpart of the other century—*sees* him ; this is the " liability he has to face." Now, years before, in *The Turn of the Screw*, James had used the same word " liability "—" liability to impressions "—in a very similar way ; he had written of the governess's " liability " to glimpses of the apparitions. That is why, when he utters the word again in these communings, he seems to catch the idea he is seeking by the " tip of the tail."

[2] " I'm glad you like adverbs—I adore them ; they are the only qualifications I really much respect, and I agree with the fine author of your quotations in saying—or in thinking—that the sense for them is *the* literary sense."—*Letters*, ed. P. Lubbock, vol. ii., p. 222.

overlooked—and a few bad moments will follow.
Generally the alarm will prove needless and he will
see—" on recovery of my wits, not to say of my wit "
—that everything is right : " I gasp with relief. . . .
Just now, a page or two back, I lost my presence of
mind, I let myself be badly scared." When he
" sees " sufficiently he will not pause to elaborate,
but will merely leave a reminder by the way—plant
a stick, as it were, to mark the spot ; but sometimes
(this happened with *The Sense of the Past*) an inter-
ruption would come in the work and he would find
that his " notation " had been insufficient. Then
would follow some searching round for the original
idea ; after a little patience as a rule it would begin
to return to him : " when I try to recover what I
so long ago had in my head about this, there glimmers out, there floats shyly back to me from afar
. . . " It is interesting, too, to accompany him in
his balancing of the pros and cons of minutiæ—ages,
appearances, chronologies—and his worries about
names. He does not wish to waste " Cantopher,"
we learn, but for a while has trouble in fitting it to
an appropriate person ; and until he has arranged
these matters to his satisfaction one character has
perforce to figure as " Aurora What's-her-name "
and another as " Mrs. So and So of Drydown,"
while a third is the " Horace Walpole man." There
are also the backgrounds to be thought out—but
they rarely seem to need much consideration : the
sense of them comes naturally to him as the story
proceeds. So, of an episode in *The Sense of the Past*
he says : " I seem to see this altogether in latish

daylight of a spring, say of a March or April, season."

The impression everywhere is of his deep joy in his craft ; the difficulties themselves are part of the joy, for he has only to press more firmly, though gently and intelligently, and all will be well. Above all, he is never satisfied until the pressure has been complete, until his theme, whatever it is, has been fully rendered. There is a title of one of James's stories that might well symbolise his constant purpose in them all : it is *The Turn of the Screw*. " The exhibitional further twist " : nothing contents him until he believes he has attained that, squeezed the best interest from his material, extracted the utmost —which is for him the refined, the deep, the ultimate meaning—from whatever he has in hand. If we compare what we have of his novel *The Sense of the Past* with the play *Berkeley Square*, adapted from it by J. L. Balderston and J. C. Squire, we shall see at a dozen points precisely what he meant by the " exhibitional further twist " ; and in these pre-liminary notes we may watch the " screw " itself turning, as he tries for " a finer twist still, a deeper depth or higher flight of the situation." He had not the special talent required for the writing of *Berkeley Square*—a good play, which has deserved its popularity ; on the other hand, he would scarcely have wished to write it : it would have seemed to him that the screw there had hardly begun to turn.

The method of the last novels is not to be summed up in a phrase : the prefaces exist to prove that ! Yet one may say that its main principle is the consistent employment of the consciousness as the medium of exposition. The change from the earlier novels is perhaps one of degree after all, but the degree is very great. The use of the consciousness is now rigorous and deliberate as it was not in any of the earlier work. There may be one consciousness framing the whole narrative, as in *The Ambassadors* ; or, as in the other two books of the final group, several minds in turn and in interplay will hold the story ; the point is that everything that now happens —or everything that really matters—is shown as mirrored in some mind. The minds are " burnished reflectors " and the beams they cast make the novel. The result (as has been pointed out) is really a special, an enlarged kind of dramatisation. Nothing is " told "—beyond unimportant details of place, time, situation and the like : we must gather for ourselves from the recorded thinkings of the characters (as in a stage drama from their speeches, looks and movements) what happens. The author's " narration " is now at a minimum : instead of narrating, he shows. It is true that James never attempted (as Joyce was later to attempt) to transfer fully to paper the moments in the brain of this or that character, as these moments might have been in actual life ; we are in contact all the time with some mind or other, but never with a whole mind in all its complex activity. James's purpose was different : from the whole stream of the consciousness he isolates the current he requires ; from the selected thinkings of his people he makes his novel.

In *The Ambassadors* only the one register is used, but the method is infinitely flexible and as a rule appropriate " reflectors " are chosen for different blocks of story ; and even within these blocks there may be—and generally are—continual slight shifts in the point of view. The closeness, too, with which the movements of any particular mind are recorded varies continually, so that we may be at one moment much more fully within it than at another : all such fluctuations are studied. But the principle of the method remains : registers there must be. So, at one point of the notes for *The Sense of the Past* James exclaims : " I, of course, under penalty of the last infamy, stick here still, as everywhere, to our knowing these things but through Ralph's knowing them." So, in the preface to *The Wings of the Dove* he speaks of Kate Croy as being, for a period in the story, " turned on " like a lamp : her mind, for a space, becomes the burnished reflector, or (he varies the image) for a time we are to " breathe through her lungs." Then Densher's mind takes up the recording. The Dove herself, though at the centre of all, is used differently, being " watched through the successive windows of other people's interest in her." But always, somewhere, is the " delegated sensibility " : for what James now wished to express—" the finer vibrations of experience "—it seemed the only method.

Its exactions are evident, and there were, besides, other obvious barriers to the general acceptance of these later books. The material itself was of the narrowest appeal : " blood and dust and heat, he ruled them out," so Mr. Wells complains ; one must agree that he did ; and there is truth in the remark of another critic that " curiosity is the one passion celebrated with any cordiality by Mr. James." It is a passion that may even assume, at times, an aspect of pitilessness ; there are stories in which that merciless æsthetic preoccupation which his characters borrow from himself seems too cold-blooded, in which their joy of curiosity, their gift of scrutiny, becomes almost appalling. Then again, his technique, as we know, was all in all to him : " the refreshment of calculation and construction " : how many phrases there are of that kind ! He speaks in one place of the management of time in the novel, of its being the job of " most difficulty and therefore of most dignity " : the " therefore " is very significant. The result sometimes—only sometimes—of such an absorption is that the work suggests excogitation, as if it were an immense technical exercise. This does not often happen, but there are moments when one has the sense of a controlling diagram into which people and their fortunes are fitted and for the purpose of which they exist. The effect, once again, is occasionally of a faint inhumanity. There are other deterrents, of which the slow time is one. The later novels move forward insensibly, with a quality almost sidereal in their motion ; certain hardly visible displace-ments occur ; the change seems slight yet—as in a regrouped constellation—can have enormous im-plications. Or we may imagine a loom furiously working to weave a great pattern which appears by

imperceptible degrees : to watch it as inch by inch
it comes needs patience.

And what happens in a late James novel ? In the
ordinary sense of the word, very little. " It is an
incident," he declared, " for a woman to stand up
with her hand resting on the table and look at you
in a certain way." These, indeed—with what they
imply—are the events, almost exclusively the events,
of the latest novels : a sudden gesture, a turn of the
eyes at a certain moment, a failure to ask a question,
a sight of two people standing at a stair-head. In
The Golden Bowl, for an example, four people are of
the first importance ; a middle-aged American, his
daughter, the Italian prince who becomes this
daughter's husband, the lady who becomes the
father's second wife : this lady and the prince, we
are to understand, had been previously lovers.
The story of the novel is the story of a gradual
regrouping of these four people, or of the slow
spiritual victory of two of them over the other two.
At no moment is any one of the characters aware of
all that is happening—there are circlings in an
obscurity, stealthy moral enmeshments—and each
of the persons concerned is alone in his or her sur-
mises, guessing dimly at what the others purpose
and know. We can hardly call it real, for it is
existence too rarified to be real, it is life infinitely—
if one will, unnaturally—intensified in a certain
direction. James knew very well, of course, what he
was about, and would have been the first to admit
that the great primary human affections were not
crudely conspicuous in a novel such as this. He was

not very eager to have them so ; but he would still have felt that it was not quite fair, after he had ruled out the " blood and dust and heat," to call what he had kept a " residuum " : for him at least this residuum—of the " finer vibrations of experience " —was precisely the value of values, the ultimate " worth-while " of life.

And surely the method itself, with all its rigours, was worth while. The demands need not be minimised—how, for a last example, the dialogue makes one strain ! In the final books it is at its subtlest, bewildering us at times as if we were in some game of blind-man's-buff—or in a labyrinth of ambiguities where we must breathe hard to follow. It is the most exacting of all James's devices and there are moments when we cry out in despair. Yet we are compelled to wonder, could the " finer vibrations " have been caught by any instrument ess delicate ?

Then there is that other instrument which he perfected in the later years and upon which he came more and more to rely—image. The later style is woven of metaphor, a shining tissue, and here at least no labours are required of us : we need only wonder and enjoy. Complex as much of the imagery is, it is with no sense of effort that it see to come : a profusion is at hand, and we never i i that it is for decoration. James now thinks in figure. It is very interesting, as one reads through those memoranda for *The Sense of the Past*, to notice how continually it is a question, not of " working out," " constructing " or " inventing," but of " seeing " :

26

again and again that word is used. And so it is with
The Golden Bowl. Towards the end of that book the
impalpable toils begin to close round the injuring
woman ; the metaphors by which her situation is
expressed vary endlessly, but James especially sees
her as a prisoner : his mind comes back constantly
to the vision of some " cage " in which Charlotte
bruises herself in vain, from which she continually
strives to escape.

" Maggie's sense (was) open as to the sight of gilt
wires and bruised wings, the spacious but suspended
cage, the home of eternal unrest, of pacings, beatings,
shakings all so vain, into which the baffled consciousness helplessly resolved itself. The cage was the
deluded condition, and Maggie, as having known
delusion—rather ! understood the nature of cages.
She walked round Charlotte's—cautiously and in a
very wide circle ; and when inevitably they had to
communicate she felt herself comparatively outside
and on the breast of nature : she saw her com-
panion's face as that of a prisoner looking through
bars. So it was that through bars, bars richly gilt
but firmly though discreetly planted, Charlotte struck
her as making a grim attempt ; from which at first
the Princess drew back as instinctively as if the door
of the cage had suddenly been opened from within."

Charlotte presently makes the attempt :

" The splendid shining supple creature was out of
the cage, was at large ; and the question now
almost grotesquely rose of whether she mightn't by
some art, just where she was and before she could go
further, be hemmed in and secured."

She *is* secured, by Verver, her husband ; and once again it is Maggie's impression that we receive, the mirror of her mind that reflects to us the situation. Her father and stepmother are walking together in the gallery at Fawns, inspecting the precious objects in their cases :

" Charlotte hung behind with emphasised attention ; she stopped when her husband stopped, but at the distance of a case or two, or of whatever other succession of objects ; and the likeness of their connection wouldn't have been wrongly figured if he had been thought of as holding in one of his pocketed hands the end of a long silken halter looped round her beautiful neck. He didn't twitch it, yet it was there ; he didn't drag her, but she came ; and those betrayals that I have described the Princess as finding irresistible in him were two or three mute facial intimations which his wife's presence didn't prevent his addressing his daughter—nor prevent his daughter, as she passed, it was doubtless to be added, from flushing a little at the receipt of. They amounted perhaps only to a wordless, wordless smile, but the smile was the soft shake of the twisted silken rope, and Maggie's translation of it, held in her breast till she got well away, came out only, as if it might have been overheard, when some door was closed behind her. ' Yes, you see—I lead her now by the neck, I lead her to her doom, and she doesn't so much as know what it is, though she has a fear in her heart which, if you had the chances to apply your ear there that I, as a husband, have, you would hear thump and thump and thump.' "

Conrad remarked that " one is never set at rest by Mr. James's novels," for they " end as an episode in life ends," that is, not very conclusively. It is true, at least of the later ones. The end is often a discord, faint or prolonged, and the definiteness even of a sharp tragic solution is lacking. But such endings, enigmatic or incomplete, can be very beautiful ; and none is more admirable in this way than that of *The Golden Bowl*. As cool twilight falls on the room in which the last scene takes place, so the close of the book itself is like a soft sinking to dusk : and in the mind, too, some shadows remain.

JAMES JOYCE

PERHAPS the readiest way of bringing the work of James Joyce into perspective, so that we may see at the outset where he stands in relation to his predecessors, is to distinguish three stages in the changing method of the English novel. Such a view will possess, needless to say, a merely diagrammatic value, for it must simplify drastically a long and intricate development, but it may serve to suggest at least a part of what has happened, and it helps, in a moment, to " place " Joyce.

Let us cast our minds back to the beginnings of the English novel, and particularly to Fielding. How does Fielding write a novel ? He writes it, to put the matter in a phrase, by telling us in person. Open *Tom Jones* at random, and unless you light upon a conversation—and no novelist in England has managed conversations more dextrously than Fielding—you are almost sure to come upon a passage like this : " Some of my readers may be inclined to think this event unnatural. [He is alluding to Tom's infidelity with Molly Seagrim.] However, the fact is true, and perhaps may be sufficiently accounted for by suggesting . . . " and so on. Fielding accounts for it very well ; he makes us understand, by his wise commentary, how natural the event was. But the interest is in the method. The author in person narrates ; he gives his authority for this and that : " The fact is true," he says. He knows what occurred, and he tells the story as if it were indeed a history and he the historian, in difficult places offering suggestions—as one better informed than we are, though not quite omniscient—concerning the motives of his people.

Here is one way of writing a novel, and when the author is a Fielding we know what an excellent way it can be. We feel his delightful presence every-where : he explains, he comments, he underlines, he warns, he jokes. The method is too good to pass into disuse. Every now and again, to-day, a really important novel of the Fielding type will appear.

Nevertheless, there have been changes. From Fielding, let us take a long leap and, passing by for the present the great mid-Victorian writers, come to the later years of the nineteenth century. No novelist of this period was more interested in his craft than Henry James, and in the method he evolved there was no place for what had been Fielding's main procedure. I have just spoken of Fielding as " giving his authority " for this and that. The word Henry James likes to use is " guarantee," and his first principle of composition is that nothing—or nothing that matters—must be given on the author's guarantee. To " tell " the reader is, he would say, to abandon the whole task of writing a novel. Instead of telling, Henry James shows, and he shows by putting us in contact with the minds of his people. When we are in contact with their minds we are in a position to judge for

31

ourselves : the author's explanations are unnecessary. Indeed, to keep himself, as author, in the background is for James a cardinal rule. He " narrates," in the ordinary sense of the word, very little ; almost all that happens (in a novel of his later period) is mirrored in the consciousness of one or other of the characters ; their minds become " burnished reflectors " ; sometimes the mind of one character will reflect the whole story.

Here, plainly, we have come a long way, in method, from Fielding. What is the next stage ? The technique of Henry James is " advanced " even for to-day, for few novelists of the present time carry his methods quite as far as he did himself. Yet a further development is possible.

Henry James, to repeat, places us in contact with the minds of his persons : but the word " contact " is not precise. It would be difficult to find even half a page in Henry James where the recorded thoughts of this or that character could have constituted an actual piece of his or her thinking as it might have been in real life. No moment, that is, in the brain of this or that character is transferred fully to paper ; rather, the thoughts are edited, selected, interpreted for us, very much as they are, say, in a Browning monologue. And just as in a Browning monologue, no matter who is speaking, the language is that of Browning, so in a Henry James novel, no matter who is thinking, the expression is in the personal style—the very definitely personal style—of Henry James. In other words, although in a late novel by Henry James we are

32

always in contact with some mind or other, it is never with a whole mind in all its complex activity ; the author, although he is now so little in evidence is still mediating ; he is still, if not patently, insidiously, between us and his people.

Can we come closer still to the minds of people in a novel ? And, instead of being given an adaptation of their thinkings, is an immediate, an exact rendering possible ? Perhaps few suspected, until Joyce wrote, how close we could get, and how precise the rendering could be. We reach the third stage in our summary scheme of technical development with the *Ulysses* of James Joyce.

Let me recall the drift of this remarkable work.

The whole action (presented in seven hundred and thirty or so very large pages) occupies approximately nineteen hours of time. It begins—the scene from first to last being in or near Dublin—at about eight o'clock in the morning of June 16th, 1904, and ends in the early hours, say between three and four, of the next day. Superficially, very little happens. This is one of the first surprises of *Ulysses* for the novel-reader, and was one of the first of the affronts it offered to the orthodox novel-writer. Arnold Bennett accused Joyce at once of having taken " malicious pleasure in picking up the first common day that came to hand," adding that he would, no doubt, if he had thought of it, have selected a day on which his hero was confined to his bed by a passing indisposition.

And, at first sight, there seems a good deal to be said for Bennett's objection. What does happen, after all ? The main character is Leopold Bloom, a canvasser for newspaper advertisements. He rises at eight o'clock, goes out to buy a kidney, comes back, takes his wife her breakfast while the kidney is cooking for his own, prepares himself for the day (he has put on black because he must attend the funeral of a friend), leaves the house. He walks along the Dublin streets rather lazily meditating ; he takes a Turkish bath (it is not even one of his busy days) ; he attends the funeral and talks with friends ; he visits a newspaper office, has a little lunch, rests at the Ormond Hotel, strolls to the beach for a breath of fresh air, and, after some further wanderings and encounters, returns to his home and goes to bed. A somewhat commonplace day in the life of the rather commonplace character, Leopold Bloom, rendered with an amplitude of detail unprecedented in literary history : it is easy to understand Bennett's protest.

Yet, he is not quite fair, nor has the rough sketch just given of the scope of the book been quite fair. At least two events of great importance were left out. One of them—Mrs. Bloom's appointment with Blazes Boylan—makes this sixteenth of June a day of considerable mental torture for Bloom ; not for long during the eighteen hours or so in which we follow him is this trouble far from his thoughts. The other event—in the design of the book the most important of all—is the meeting of Bloom and Stephen Dedalus. It is a meeting that profoundly affects both lives, for each man is enabled by it to find himself : Bloom, because he can, in a sense, regain in Stephen the son whom he lost long ago ; Stephen, because (as a creative artist) he has encountered in Bloom his predestined subject.

For both of these men, therefore, the day is really important, and even if we were still to quarrel with the work for the " lack of distinction " in its matter, it would remain true that few books leave us with the sensation of having been plunged so deeply into life. This leads us to a consideration of its method, for it is by his unusual technique that Joyce is able to create such an impression.

I say " method," and it is true that Joyce holds one objective before him. He is trying to find the complete and accurate way of rendering his subject, or of this or that part of it with which he is at the moment dealing. But such a search means, in the result, that his treatment varies from episode to episode, though one device, modified in several ways, is of quite outstanding importance.

The book begins, not at all startlingly, like an orthodox novel : the texture of the first few pages, which introduce us to Stephen Dedalus, is quite ordinary. But presently we become aware of a change. What Stephen is doing, what he is saying, begin almost at once to dwindle in importance ; we even lose our grip a little of these matters ; and something else increasingly takes their place—what he is thinking. There is no other word to use but that, but it means now the kind of thinking that actually does go on in our minds from moment to moment, not the *arranged* thinking of a character in Henry James. Thus, we hear him at his school, giving lessons ; we hear the questions of the boys and his replies ; but we overhear, as well, his unspoken meditations, abrupt, unpredictable, many of them bitter, inward-turning, for he has had a troubled spiritual history and is now at odds with his life. Stephen's mind is subtle, his nature proud, fastidious and lonely, his temperament that of an artist ; and his thoughts, as they come, make a very intricate, sometimes a very beautiful, pattern.

Leopold Bloom's mind is simpler, but interesting in its way. He is an Irish Jew, thirty-eight years of age, and a man of a type not often found within the pages of a novel. This is because, by ordinary methods, he would be difficult to treat. His nature is negative. Thus, he loves his wife, yet, knowing of her infidelities, makes no move to interfere : it is rather humility than cowardice that restrains him. Again, he is a friendless man ; he is quiet and unassuming, yet his Dublin acquaintances do not much care for him, though they are forced to respect certain of his qualities. He has a real kindliness of disposition ; as he helps the blind piano-tuner across the road he gropes for a word or two that will be sympathetic and yet tactful : " Say something to him. Better not do the condescending . . . Poor fellow, quite a boy." His brain, too, is good, scientifically bent and reasonably well-stocked with information. Yet we ourselves, who come to know him far better than his closest associates could have done, hardly reach the point of liking him, though we do not actively dislike him ; and perhaps the reason for the feeling we have towards him is that he impresses us in some vague general way, as well as in certain precise and definite ways, as ignoble.

But I suppose that few commentators find it easy to sum up Leopold Bloom, and the difficulty is not fully accounted for by the indefinite character of the man. It is explained also, paradoxically, by this, that we know so very much about him. In fiction, the sharply remembered people are very often the people of whose natures we are shown only a small part, the people whose characters are drastically selected for us ; and of course it is easy to under· stand why it should be so. What fictitious personage lives in our mind more vividly than Mr. Micawber ? How easy to sum up Mr. Micawber ! We know so little about him, but we know that little so well. It is not so easy to sum up Hamlet, or rather everybody sums him up differently ; and it is partly because our knowledge of him is so various and full. But let us go a stage farther. How would one proceed to sum up one's own character ? This is quite a different thing from having it summed up for one ; most of us can easily guess how such characterisations go, and are prepared (a little ruefully, it may be) to admit that they represent fairly accurately the simplified truth of the matter. Only, we ourselves have so much more information that we do not find it so easy to simplify ; we are in possession of too much material, really, for a clear and satisfactory picture of ourselves.

It is like that with our knowledge of Leopold Bloom in *Ulysses*. It has been said that " we know more about him than we know about any other character in fiction," and it would be difficult to deny the justice of this claim. We know practically everything he thinks about for eighteen hours, and that means that we know virtually all there is to know of him.

The stupendousness of this really needs to be dwelt upon. Leaving aside for the moment the question whether Bloom's thoughts are worth having, or whether, as Bennett considered, the net result of all this material is a " pervading difficult dullness," the achievement in itself—as a creative feat—takes one's breath away. The method—not invented by Joyce, but never employed before on such a scale—is that of the " interior " or mental monologue. Joyce uses a notation, in Bloom's case rather abrupt, staccato, to suggest the thoughts of the man just as they come, twisting this way and that as sights catch his eye, rouse memories, provoke associations ; we follow instant by instant the crazy trail of the man's mind. Now, we are all, of course, familiar with these processes ; we know how our own thoughts skip and jump here and there, and can travel in a few bounds from one end of the world to the other. Bloom's mind does the same. He is walking, for example, by the riverside, when someone puts an evangelical leaflet into his hand ; it is because of this incident that a few seconds afterwards he is thinking of Malaga raisins. The train of thought is as follows : the leaflet reminds him of Torry and Alexander ; " paying game," he meditates ; some Birmingham firm, he remembers, rigged up a luminous crucifix once, used phosphorus, probably.

The idea of phosphorus starts another recollection, reminding him of a time he saw phosphorescence in a fish, " bluey-silver " it was. He had gone down to the pantry and saw the codfish gleaming in the dark ; his wife had asked him to bring her up some Malaga raisins.

A little later he notices sea-gulls wheeling and buys two Banbury cakes to feed them ; the gulls lead his mind by devious routes to Robinson Crusoe—a quotation will show the style. He " broke the brittle paste and threw its fragments down into the Liffey. See that ? The gulls swooped silently, two, then all, from their heights, pouncing on prey. Gone. Every morsel.

" Aware of their greed and cunning he shook the powdery crumb from his hands. They never expected that. Manna. Live on fishy flesh they have to, all sea birds, gulls, seagoose. Swans from Anna Liffey swim down here sometimes to preen themselves. No accounting for tastes. Wonder what kind is swan meat. Robinson Crusoe had to live on them."

So his thoughts flow, not always lazily like this. Every now and again emotion, or remembered emotion, will quicken them, and the sight of Boylan, whose path crosses his several times during the day, always brings a sudden swirl and tumult into them, a momentary panic.

It strikes one at first as perhaps not very difficult, this recording of trains of thought, and neither, in itself, is it. We can each of us do it any minute by merely taking up a pencil. But try to do it for someone else, for an imaginary person, and then, page after page, keep the pattern coherent, recording, not any train, but the one particular train that is right for this, out of all other personalities, in these and no other circumstances. For grasp of character, at least, no test can be conceived more severe.

As far as one can judge, there is no breakdown in the record given by Joyce of Leopold Bloom. That is another way of saying that Bloom's mind, after a time, acquires for us an identity ; after a little experience we begin to recognise his way of thinking. It is utterly different from the way of Stephen Dedalus, or of his wife, or of anyone else, and the sensation of being quite within a mind in this fashion—not partially, but completely within—is very curious. Indeed, the effect at a first reading of *Ulysses* is not a little bewildering. It is bewildering, in the first place, because the mind exists for us, for a while, apart from a body, for it is not until some time has elapsed that we begin to learn, from information picked up here and there, what Bloom looks like ; and the sensation of sharing the thoughts of a man whom one cannot picture to oneself is very curious. Then, it takes time to gain one's bearings in the outside world, and this, too, if one thinks of it, is easily understood. When we walk along a familiar street, or enter a room we know well, we do not notice very particularly objects we have seen hundreds of times before. If someone else could be in my mind as I entered my study, that person would gain a very poor idea indeed of what my study looked like, simply because my mind would not be very consciously occupied with it. So, Bloom's mind does not reflect to us a very good picture at all of his kitchen as he prepares his breakfast; he moves about, performing certain actions, but the surroundings are rather hazy to us. It is the same with the Dublin streets. This or that object, as he goes along, enters his thoughts, but we cannot expect him to introduce us to the street in which he is walking, as a novelist might. Joyce himself helps now and then with " stage-directions," but it is part of his plan to keep his intrusions, as author, as infrequent as may be. Still, we find that the Dublin scene, after a while, has invaded our consciousness. We rarely *see* it, because Bloom himself only at moments looks at it with full awareness; for most of the time it is a background to his thoughts; but it is a very real background, and so it comes to be for us.

Occasionally, however, the scene will become much more vivid; we see, suddenly, very much more; and this is generally because we are shifted to a place where the characters whose minds we possess grow, for some reason, more conscious of their surroundings. The episode at the beach (*Nausikaa*) illustrates this very well. Here sights and sounds are noticed more, for the people have come down in the evening for pastime and relaxation, and yield themselves in this interval of leisure to enjoyment of the hour and the place.

But this episode, besides, is extremely interesting for its method. During its course we are for half the time, but only half, in the mind of Leopold Bloom.

For the other half we are amongst the thoughts of Gerty MacDowell, who has come with two girl friends to have a " cosy chat beside the sparkling waves and discuss matters feminine." Gerty Mac-Dowell has a romantic mind which has been nourished on cheap fiction, and the surroundings soon affect her mood. She begins to notice Bloom (sitting not far off), to speculate about him, and presently to construct a sentimental story, involving the two of them, in the manner of the novelettes of which she is so fond. The vocabulary of her mono-logue is drawn from at least two distinct sources. There is first her own personal " chit-chat " style, her every-day girlish dialect with its homely proverbs, its stock phrases and the like : the very it, split your sides, every inch a gentleman, something off the common, little love of a hat, a deliberate lie, their little tiffs, honour where honour is due. But her mind, also, is crammed with expressions from the novels she reads, and in her present wistful, dreamy mood they afford her a natural means of utterance : winsome Irish girlhood, waxen pallor, rosebud mouth, a gentlewoman of high degree, eyes of witchery, haunting expression, crowning glory, wealth of wonderful hair.

So, as she sits there by the waters of the bay she creates for herself the part of a sad heroine of romance : " Had kind fate but willed her to be born a gentlewoman of high degree in her own right and had she only received the benefit of a good education Gerty MacDowell might easily have held her own beside any lady in the land." Then her thoughts—and in this passage the mingling of styles is very evident—include the strange gentleman sitting a few yards away : " She could see at once by his dark eyes and his pale intellectual face that he was a foreigner the image of the photo she had of Martin Harvey, the matinée idol, only for the moustache which she preferred because she wasn't stage-struck like Winny Rippingham that wanted they two to always dress the same on account of a play but she could not see whether he had an aquiline nose or slightly *retroussé* from where she was sitting. He was in deep mourning, she could see that, and the story of a haunting sorrow was written on his face. She would have given worlds to know what it was."

In the Gerty MacDowell monologue Joyce's gift of mimicry is triumphantly employed. The novelettes that she reads have helped to form Gerty's mind; her imagination has been fed upon them so that they have now become a part of her ; and by imitating their manner and mixing it with her native untutored idiom Joyce is able to convey, with a completeness perhaps not possible otherwise, the very texture of her thinking. The device is truly expressive here.

But it is always prudent to be a little on one's guard against Joyce when he is writing parodies. He has such skill in them, and obviously enjoys the exercise so much, that one suspects he might on occasion be tempted into indulging his gift even were it not strictly in place. It is clear that at least once in *Ulysses* he has been so tempted.

JAMES, JOYCE, AND OTHERS

During the course of his day Bloom visits a maternity hospital ; he calls to obtain news of Mrs. Purefoy and is invited by the young house surgeon, Dixon, to a room where medical students and others are gathered for talk and refreshment. The episode is rendered in a series of parodies of the prose styles of English literature. The chapter is very enjoyable and, as a feat of virtuosity, would perhaps be difficult to equal. We have reminiscences of alliterative Old English—" Before born babe bliss had. Within womb won he worship "—then, paragraph by paragraph, are led through the phases of English prose as it evolves, listening to the voices of Malory, Milton, Browne, Bunyan, Pepys, Swift, up to Ruskin and Pater and beyond, as in turn they take up the story. The whole episode is a treasury of its kind. The voices " come through " amazingly, so that we have starts of delighted recognition as this one or that one begins. When it is time for the birth of the babe to be announced and for the father to be congratulated, a voice, louder than any we have heard before, suddenly clangs out ; the first syllables are familiar ; we listen, and in an instant have recognised it : the unmistakable ringing tones of Carlyle are pronouncing a benediction : " God's air, the Allfather's air, scintillant, circumambient, cessile air. Breathe it deep into thee ! By heaven, Theodore Purefoy, thou hast done a doughty deed . . . "

But what is the purport in the book of this series of clever imitations ? Do the parodies really serve a purpose ? It cannot for a moment be maintained that they do. The history of the evolution of English prose in a far-fetched way matches the development of the human embryo, but it is obvious that such a correspondence has no real point. The truth is that Joyce's delight in a certain technical exercise has here only the frailest pretext to justify it.

There is a second episode in the book against which, perhaps, much the same sort of criticism applies. It is near the end. Bloom, after a tiring day—a day that, for all its humdrum air, has brought him a good deal of fatiguing emotional experience—has ended by following Stephen Dedalus to the quarter of the city known as Nighttown, and, after some time spent in the place, has emerged with his friend into the open. They walk slowly towards the cabman's shelter near Butt Bridge. Reaction is on them both. It is a time of the night, or morning —the small hours—when vitality is low ; physically and mentally they are worn out. The passage is a long one and is given in a prose as full of weariness and flaccidity as the theme. " Preparatory to anything else Mr. Bloom brushed off the greater bulk of the shavings and handed Stephen the hat and ash plant and bucked him up generally in orthodox Samaritan fashion, which he very badly needed." So this formless worn-out prose continues. What Joyce does is to imitate the kind of English in which every phrase is stereotyped—the kind of English that O. Henry satirised in his story *Calloway's Code*. Like the reporter in that story we can guess the second of any pair of words from the first : highly advisable, confidently anticipated, time-honoured

45

adage, blissfully unconscious, cordially disliked, vexed question. Now and again we are given an alternative and might be wrong in our guess. Thus the " highly " just quoted went with " advisable " ; a little later it goes with " providential." But duties always devolve, footsteps always lag, and if circumstances are unfavourable one always finds oneself " handicapped " by them.

Joyce's workmanship is, no doubt, as deft here as anywhere in *Ulysses* and the episode is full of humour, but such a treatment surely has its perils. To present weariness in a way that may itself so soon become wearisome ; to express dullness dully ; in practice, at any rate, the method might quickly prove unworkable.

Such examples, however, prove Joyce a writer of manifold inventiveness and of the richest technical resource : a writer, also, who takes a good deal of pleasure in ingenuity for its own sake. Apart from the " heroically laboured " Odyssean parallel, there are many indications of such pleasure in his own comments upon his work and in certain explanations he has given. And perhaps, too, his very mastery of words leads him at times to attempt what is nearly, by the nature of the case, impossible.

Let me give an example of a kind rather different from the passages we have so far considered. Joyce is said to have taken keen enjoyment in composing the episode of *The Sirens ;* his enjoyment, if only because of his own passion for music, was natural, for this is the musical episode. The scene is the bar of the Ormond Hotel ; the sirens themselves are the two maids, Miss Douce and Miss Kennedy. Bloom enters the hotel at about four o'clock in the afternoon ; we are in his consciousness occasionally during the episode, not continually. We receive impressions of the talk, the lights, the glitter, and certain events of importance for Bloom take place. But what is most interesting is the method by which Joyce renders the scene. He tries to convey it all— the feeling of the time and place, the tiredness growing on Bloom so that his senses are becoming a little blurred, the warmth, the fading afternoon, the sounds entering from outside : some of them, like the jingling of Blazes Boylan's jaunting-car, very significant—by making a musical pattern of words. The episode is intricately composed, with themes that recur and alter, the themes here being key-phrases. Most of them are announced to us before the episode begins, for at the head of the chapter we come upon a series of disconnected and fragmentary sentences, in themselves quite insoluble :

Bronze by gold heard the hoofirons, steelyringing . . .
Blew. Blue bloom is on the
Gold pinnacled hair . . .
Lost. Throstle fluted. All is lost now . . .

The text which follows makes these broken words plain. They are almost exactly equivalent (a pretty example, which has been noted, of Joyce's love of an ingenious completeness) to the sounds which float out from an orchestra before the real playing begins : disjointed excerpts from the piece which is to come, a bar here, a bar there, as this or that instrument is tried. And just as at a concert these preliminary snatches grow presently into coherence, so in *The Sirens* the opening sentence of the chapter clarifies for us the first of the fragments we have just read : " Bronze by gold, Miss Douce's head by Miss Kennedy's head, over the crossblind of the Ormond bar heard the viceregal hoofs go by, ringing steel."

The evocative quality in the language is evident, and all through this passage one notes the unusual resonance that words seem to acquire. It is partly because *sound* is dominant in the subject-matter : a tuning-fork yields its throbbing call, Simon Dedalus sings (" Tenderness it welled : slow, swelling . . . "), Miss Douce trills to herself, coins ring on the counter, bottles are " popcorked," the cash register clangs, hoof-beats echo sharply, the car of Boylan jingles jauntily over the bridge. One does not, I think, after reading this episode, have a very clear picture of anything ; the scene is rather a coloured blur : there are flashes from mirrors, glints from glasses, reflections from gold and bronze hair, but all in a haze, indistinct. Our ears, however, are receiving the sharpest impressions all the time. The care that has gone into the passage is very striking, and, as usual, Joyce has not been able to refrain from inserting a gratuitous parody or two, in harmony with the general idea : he burlesques, here and there, the rhythms of light popular music. But, in the more serious parts, the method is sustained from start to finish. The full ingenuity of the performance is not, perhaps, to be appreciated without expert musical knowledge, but some of the sound-effects are impressive even to the amateur. The bronze-gold motif is especially interesting, reappearing in these forms :

> Yes, bronze from anear, by gold from afar, heard steel from anear, hoofs ring from afar, and heard steelhoofs ringhoof ringsteel.

Again (the maids burst into laughter, their broken references to the joke appearing in the description) :

> In a giggling peal young goldbronze voices blended, Douce with Kennedy your other eye. They threw young heads back, bronze gigglegold, to let freefly their laughter, screaming, your other, . . .

And again their merriment described :

> Shrill, with deep laughter, after bronze in gold, they urged each other to peal after peal, ringing in changes, bronzegold, goldbronze, shrilldeep, to laughter after laughter.

It will be seen, then, with what varied approaches Joyce comes to his problem, or his problems, for every section sets him a new task and he exerts himself to find the one fitting treatment. There are devices which I have not space even to mention, but two episodes remain which demand at least a word, for they are amongst the most remarkable in the book : even the sceptical Arnold Bennett was moved by them to admiring astonishment. They are the Nighttown scene, or, to give it its Odyssean name, the episode of *Circe ;* and the monologue which concludes the work, the unuttered meditation of Marion Bloom, or, to give it its Odyssean name, the episode of *Penelope*.

The first is a dramatic phantasmagoria which has reminded nearly everyone of the *Walpurgisnacht* in *Faust*. Stephen and Bloom come together again in the low haunts of Nighttown ; it is late, they have both experienced much, suffered much, during the day ; they are very tired. Their minds are ready for fantasy. They have reached a point where the line between external reality and the images conjured up by their own brains begins to waver. They see what is before their eyes (though they see it often distorted), but they also see phantoms, the wraiths of their own fears, hopes, secret desires, memories, impressions of the past day. All these intangible shapes, these figments of the overwrought brain, become *dramatis personæ*, for it is the principle of hallucination that dominates the scene. Stephen's own experiences reach their culmination with the appearance of the image of his dead mother ; all day he has been haunted by the memory of her, has been tortured (in spite of his judgment) by a sense of guilt in having refused her last request. The terrible simulacrum " comes nearer, breathing upon him softly her breath of wetted ashes." Stephen's endurance gives way, his features " grow drawn and grey and old," and presently with a wild gesture he sweeps down the chandelier. The crash is like the end of the world : " Time's livid final flame leaps and, in the following darkness, ruin of all space, shattered glass and toppling masonry." Stephen rushes into the night, but Bloom finds him and, with a father's care, pilots him to the cabman's shelter and then to his own home : Telemachus and Ulysses have found each other.

We come, after a while, to the last episode in the book. Bloom climbs wearily into bed, falls asleep, and we are left alone—with the mind of Mrs. Bloom.

We have seen how Joyce varies according to the person his way of recording these thought-streams ; the method he adopts for Marion Bloom is different from any yet used. It is a heavy, turbid, relentless flood, a great tide of thought that is almost equally sensation, and her whole life seems in it. Images of past, present and future mingle : her early days at Gibraltar, her first meeting with Bloom, her late dissatisfactions, her new loves, hopes, worries : everything significant in her experience seethes up as her mind goes churning on. We may quarrel with other sections of *Ulysses*, feel dubious here and discouraged there, but this last chapter is plainly a masterpiece of its kind. It is also one of the least difficult ; indeed, the only source of trouble at all, and it is slight, is the complete absence of punctuation. Marion Bloom's " non-stop monologue " (the phrase is Mr. Budgen's) covers forty-two large pages, and, apart from a few paragraph divisions (where her thoughts themselves seem to pause for breath) there is no pointing of any kind. Her mind is like that : Bloom's mind darts hither and thither, but Mrs. Bloom's mind endlessly unrolls. If we take into account the paragraph divisions, then we could describe her monologue (again with Mr. Budgen) as consisting of " eight unpunctuated sentences of about five thousand words each." To read it is to know Mrs. Bloom through and through and for ever and ever. The book *Ulysses* is a world, and this monologue is a world within a world. Joyce himself has commented justly on his achievement here. Marion Bloom's monologue, he says, " turns slowly, evenly, though with variations, capriciously, but surely like the huge earth ball itself round and round spinning " ; and so it does. I suppose no technical device used in *Ulysses* is so secure as that of the interior monologue ; it seems fitting that the book should close with so triumphant an example of the method. No representation of a human mind could well be more intimate, more thorough, than this.

Or could it ? Is it possible to penetrate deeper still ? Is a fourth stage in our provisional scheme even imaginable ? Only if the representation, passing beneath the conscious life, should enter the realm of dreams ; and Joyce is even now, it appears, striving to effect this very passage. He is at present, as we know, working on a " something " even harder to classify than *Ulysses ;* only fragments have been published ; the " Work " is " in Progress." But it has to do, it would seem, not with a waking mind at all, not with one man's day, but with one man's night—with a sleep. The difficulties in this new work—the word-play, the allusiveness, the " condensation," all the intricacies of the dream-language —are far beyond those of *Ulysses*, and whether anybody but Joyce himself will ever properly understand it remains at the moment dubious. Happily we need not for the present decide. We can wait and see.

THOMAS HARDY AND 'THE DYNASTS'

HARDY has a stray observation (it is recorded by Mrs. Hardy in the *Early Life*) which expresses perfectly the guiding principle of his art. He wrote : " As in looking at a carpet, by following one colour a certain pattern is suggested, by following another colour, another ; so in life the seer should watch that pattern among general things which his idiosyncrasy moves him to observe, and describe that alone. This is, quite accurately, a going to Nature ; yet the result is no mere photograph, but purely a product of the writer's own mind." That is what Hardy had been doing in the series of novels that ended in 1896 with *Jude the Obscure*—seven years before the appearance of the first part of *The Dynasts :* he had been working out " that pattern among general things which his idiosyncrasy moved him to observe." We know the colour in life that caught his eye and determined the pattern. His bent appeared very early. Even the idyllic *Under the Greenwood Tree*—his inaugural piece, properly speaking—ends with a touch of irony, the secret that Fancy would " never tell." There is a faintly ominous quality in this conclusion, as if the author were hinting : " Here is a fresh and dainty little novel ; but do not imagine that I believe that life is really like this, or that I could not, easily, have

made a very different book out of my subject."
From now on the tone steadily deepens : one recalls
his own phrase, " a good look at the worst " : his
scrutiny, as the novels proceed, becomes ever more
unblinking.

It is very interesting to watch this gradual darkening of tone in the six major novels he was now to
write (I leave out of account books in the lighter
style, such as *The Trumpet-Major* and *Two on a
Tower*, which, with all their charm, plainly do not
carry the full burden of what he had to say). The
first of the main line is *Far from the Madding Crowd*,
a pastoral, its essence, as the very names of the
chapters show—The Malthouse, The Sheep-Wash-
ing, Hiving the Bees—in its delectable representation of the routine of country life. Yet into the
golden scene tragedy intrudes ; humanity is shown
suffering ; Gabriel and Bathsheba themselves reach
their happiness through pain and trial and with
spirits notably subdued. In the next novel the
tragic significance is definitely central. Yet *The
Return of the Native* is still, in feeling, a long way
from *Jude the Obscure*. It is not a distressing tragedy,
and one main reason surely is that we have a sense
of justice in the development. Eustacia, besides—
she of the " flame-like " soul—is not the kind of
heroine to be pitied. How she would resent that !
She is a splendid creature who has had her chance,
and who has been vanquished in fair fight with the
universe. She has been defeated, but she has lived
her life (" a blaze of love, and extinction ") with
defiance and with glory. In *The Mayor of Caster-*

54

bridge the impression of justice is even stronger, and, again, the chief character has real tragic power. In this novel, more evidently than in its predecessor, far more conspicuously than in any other novel of Hardy's, fate is felt as within a personality. Henchard (the most forceful character of Hardy's drawing) is self-destroyed ; but the conflict has been on an impressive scale, and the end still leaves us feeling the innate strength of the man. His punishment, fearful as it is, is not greater than he can bear. In both these novels humanity is represented as powerful, as being, in a way, a match for destiny. But now this sense of power (and therefore of responsibility) in the human combatants begins to diminish. The design of *The Woodlanders*, the next book, has some resemblance to that of *Far from the Madding Crowd* ; but what a difference in the mood ! Here, almost from the first lines, we have a premonition of sad fatality. Fortunes turn awry, and we know, from something in the very air of those damp and lonely woodlands, that they must. For the woods themselves are like a symbol : it is in their autumnal guise that we chiefly remember them and in their aspects of saddening decay. Nor are there characters here of the rich vitality of Eustacia, the crude vigour of Henchard. Poor Winterborne—the genius of the scene, " Autumn's very brother "—is ineffectual to cope with baffling circumstance ; from the first, we felt that he was marked for mischance. But the change, in the next novel, is still more definite, and it is a change, above all, in the author's attitude. It sounds in the chal-

55

lenging title, *Tess of the D'Urbervilles*, "a Pure Woman faithfully presented by Thomas Hardy." The note that rings in this book—and we have heard it in no previous novel of Hardy's—is that of anger : indignation at the powers in control of human lives, powers here felt as outside humanity and alien to it. A passionate defensiveness unites the author with this heroine ; he would protect her ; as it is, he indicts savagely the Wrong of which she is victim. As for the fairness, here, of the conflict—the idea is laughable. There are passages in the book which sound like taunts of the Beings who do such things, or let such things happen, and there are jibes at the poets of optimism ; like this : " To Tess, as to not a few million of others, there was ghastly satire in the poet's lines—

> not in utter nakedness,
> But trailing clouds of glory do we come " ;

or like this : " In the anguish of his heart he quoted a line from a poet, with peculiar emendations of his own :

> God's *not* in His heaven ; all's *wrong* with the world."

The virtual motto of the novel—the lines are quoted in the preface—is Gloster's outraged cry in *King Lear :*

> As flies to wanton boys are we to the gods :
> They kill us for their sport ;

and there are images that seem to underline the text, like the picture of Tess " standing still upon the hemmed expanse of verdant flatness, like a fly on a billiard table, and of no more consequence to the surroundings than that fly."

Yet we all know the beauty of this bitter novel. Hardy often spoke of the transmuting quality of art —its power to glorify pain, nay, ugliness itself. His own art, too, had that magic. The loveliness of Tess's nature, and the loveliness of the scenes—the two vales, the one with its deep blue atmosphere, the other with its ethereal mists of dawn—irradiate the book.

In the last of the series this transfiguring beauty is not so evident. Hardy could make his titles very telling, and no story or poem was named more bitingly than this novel. It was called once, satirically, *The Simpletons ;* again, with stirring resonance, *Hearts Insurgent ;* its final grim name was *Jude the Obscure.* Here, amidst the suffering and the squalor, the last gleams of the exaltation of tragedy are extinguished ; or perhaps not quite, even yet, for mankind, though so pitifully pictured, is still noble, and the glow of those two fruitlessly aspiring " hearts insurgent "—the divine enthusiasm of " the simpletons "—is not quenched till life itself goes. Still, the shadows cast by the frowning universe have become black indeed ; face to face with this monstrous indifference in things, man has no hope.

Hardy published *Jude the Obscure* (to the tune of much protesting outcry) in 1896, and he wrote no more novels, or none that matters. He had described the pattern of human experience in the way in which to his idiosyncrasy it presented itself. But he had still something to say, though not in prose fiction. In a great poem, with its liberating symbolisms, he believed he could convey more of what was in his heart than any novel had ever given him freedom to express. After *Jude* came two books of verse ; then, in 1903, the first volume of *The Dynasts*. In a late chapter of *Jude*, Hardy had described the " vague and quaint imaginings " that in earlier days had haunted Sue : the idea " that the world resembled a stanza or melody composed in a dream ; it was wonderfully excellent to the half-aroused intelligence, but hopelessly absurd at the full waking ; that the First Cause worked automatically like a somnambulist, and not reflectively like a sage." To this " Somnambulist First Cause " Hardy's thoughts had been gathering for many years. Now he would proceed to the demonstration and trace the *full* pattern of life as it struck his eyes.

In a sense the picture he was now to draw is more terrible than any that had appeared in the novels, even in the last. In *Jude* mankind, though obscure, may still be represented by two puny figures, vainly struggling. But in *The Dynasts* poor " pitpatting " humanity has dwindled to an insignificance far beyond that. No individual—not even Napoleon, in spite of Hardy's first thoughts—has sufficient import to be the hero of this work : nearly as well single out an ant from the myriads of its kind. On the other hand, the bitterness of the two concluding novels disappears. Hardy no longer rages, is no longer resentful. With calm spirit, with compassion, but with inexorable fidelity to his vision, he comes to his mighty drama of the Breaking of Nations, which is also his most explicit utterance of all that he most deeply felt about the nature of things. *The Dynasts*, in this way and others, is Hardy's central, his crowning, work.

First, as to its form. Hardy did not reach a decision about this quite at once. A note belonging to 1875—for the ambition had been long cherished —is expressed like this : " A Ballad of the Hundred Days. Then another of Moscow. Others of earlier campaigns—forming altogether an Iliad of Europe from 1789 to 1815." The idea of a chain of ballads, however, was soon abandoned. A memorandum two years later runs as follows : " Consider a grand drama, based on the wars with Napoleon, or some one campaign. . . . It might be called ' Napoleon ' or ' Josephine ' or by some other person's name." A grand drama : this is only 1877, and it is clear that the essential plan is already in Hardy's grasp. He hesitated a little, however, even yet, and in 1881 reverted temporarily to the scheme of an " Homeric Ballad in which Napoleon is a sort of Achilles." But this was only a belated echo of his original notion, for in the same month in which he wrote that note he also wrote this, a very firm statement, in which for the first time there is a glimpse of the underlying idea : " Mode for an historical drama. Action mostly automatic ; reflex movement, etc. Not the result of what is called motive, though always ostensibly so, even to the actors' own consciousness." By the next year (February, 1882) he has a clear perception of what is to be the core of the work : " Write a history of human automatism or impulsion, viz., an account of human action in spite of human knowledge, showing how very far conduct lags behind the knowledge that should really guide it." But the plan was to go on maturing in his mind for twenty years yet ; not until 1903 (as we have seen) was the first volume published.

And even then Hardy did not know quite how to describe it. " A Drama of the Napoleonic Wars " was the sub-title he adopted at the time, though he explained that he meant it as a drama " for mental performance " only. Later, when the second and third parts appeared, it was called an Epic-Drama, a name which gives a better suggestion of the majestic scope of the completed work. But the unsatisfactoriness of the available terminology is still emphasised by the first words of the preface, where Hardy speaks of " The Spectacle here presented in the likeness of a Drama." There was, in fact, no word precisely to fit it—*was*, because, in a sense, we are in a better position to describe the work (I mean, to describe the form of it) than Hardy himself. This is what, without knowing it, he had written in *The Dynasts*—it is no wonder he was baffled to find a suitable term : he had written a super-scenario for an imaginary super-film (a film " for mental exhibition " only).

To illustrate this description. *The Dynasts*—this Epic-Drama in three parts, nineteen acts, and one hundred and thirty scenes—begins and ends, it will be remembered, in what Hardy calls the Overworld, a region corresponding to Milton's Heaven or Homer's Olympus. The celestial machinery here, however, is thrillingly modern, and the Beings who speak are the abstractions of modern thought—or of Hardy's modern thought—impersonated as Phantom Intelligences. One set of these, the Chorus of the Pities, approximates (the author explains) to the " Universal Sympathy of human nature." The others have various easily discerned significances. There is the Ancient Spirit of the Years ; there is the Shade of the Earth ; there are the Spirits Sinister and Ironic. This assemblage, from its eyrie, observes and discusses the human action. But this eyrie, which we, as co-observers share, is no fixed summit of Olympus. It is an infinitely movable point in space—it is, in fact, the eye of a super-camera. Our very first view from it, which is also to be our last, is stupendous, and characteristic. Hardy describes it : " The nether sky opens, and Europe is disclosed as a prone and emaciated figure, the Alps shaping like a backbone, and the branching mountain-chains like ribs, the peninsular plateau of Spain forming a head." We are given, in fact, a panorama of the continent from Spain to the Arctic Ocean, and from France to the " cloud-combed " Urals. Now, after this opening aerial prospect, the imaginary camera moves : it advances towards its object. Hardy says : " The point of view then sinks downwards through space, and draws near to the surface of the perturbed countries, where the peoples, distressed by events which they did not cause, are seen writhing, heaving and

vibrating in their various cities and nationalities."
The Fore Scene over, the locality alters abruptly.
We find ourselves on a ridge in Wessex, listening to
the passengers of a stage coach talking of Boney.
Then, in succession, we shift to the Ministry of
Marine at Paris, to the House of Commons, to
Boulogne, to Milan, the view sometimes narrowing
to an interior, or beyond that to a " close-up," so
that we can study the expression of Napoleon's
features, sometimes taking its vantage in the middle
air. There is a continual " fading-out "—and
" fading-in." " Clouds," Hardy will say, " gather
over the scene and slowly open elsewhere." [1] The

---

[1] Occasionally the scenes " shut," merely, but as a rule fade—in
haze, rain, sea-mist, the murk of evening : " the scene darkens,"
" the scene over-clouds," " the night-shades close over," " a nebulous
curtain draws slowly across." The fading is often the imaginative
completion of the scene. At the end of the Fourth Act of the Second
Part the Chorus of Pities echoes the lamentation of the English
soldiers rotting upon " the ever wan morass " of Walcheren :

> O ancient Delta, where the fen-lights flit !
> Ignoble sediment of loftier lands,
> Thy humour clings about our hearts and hands
> And solves us to its softness, till we sit
> As we were part of it.

Each creeping day creeping files of soldiers carry their dead to
burial—

> Bearing them to their lightless last asile
> Where weary wave-wails from the clammy shore
> Will reach their ears no more.

They themselves linger, fading like the mist, soon—

> by this pale sea
> To perish silently.

The scene ends with the direction : " The night fog enwraps the
isle and the dying English army."
The fading is sometimes accompanied by recession, the scene
dwindling into a miniature : " The point of view recedes, the whole
fabric [of Milan Cathedral] smalling into distance, and becoming

whole effect, the vision now swooping towards the point of focus with lightning velocity, now taking in a panorama through an immense arc, and always advancing in time, is unique (surely) in literature and can be strangely impressive. Such a scene as that of the retreat from Moscow, so viewed, seems to acquire new pathos. Here, at first, the point of observation is high amongst shifting clouds, the earth a mere " confused expanse " below. Through the rifts we behold, pitifully diminished in the great perspective, the line of the Army " once called the Grand." A flake of snow floats down on it, then another and another, till " all is phantasmal grey and white." Small objects are detached from the caterpillar shape :

> These atoms that drop off are snuffed-out souls
> Who are enghosted by the caressing snow.

" Endowed with enlarged powers of audition as of vision [if that is not sound-film, what is ?], we are struck by the mournful taciturnity that prevails. Nature is mute. . . . With growing nearness more is revealed." Marshal Ney, as we come closer, is recognised, and Napoleon himself is discerned " amid the rest, marching on foot through the snow-flakes." We see what the soldiers are wearing.

like a rare, delicately carved alabaster ornament." Sounds, too, fade : " The confused tongues of the assembly [at a London house] waste away into distance, till they are heard but as the babblings of the sea from a high cliff, the scene becoming small and indistinct therewith. This passes into silence, and the whole disappears." Sometimes a faint sound remains, like " the soft hiss of the rain that falls impartially on both the sleeping armies," in the night before Waterloo.

Now the army approaches a river—it is the Beresina —and, that we may observe the engagement at the bridges, "the point of vision descends to earth, close to the scene of action."

I may refer, briefly, to two other scenes. The first is not, in itself, very significant, but includes a visual effect which has become, of late, very familiar to us. We are on the road to Waterloo, watching the English troops moving back from Quatre Bras, and the way in which we watch them is interesting. We observe them as if through the lens of a pursuing camera, so that the fields and hedges slip by us on either side as we keep up with the rear of the column. "The focus of the scene follows the retreating English army, the highway and its margins panoramically gliding past the vision of the spectator."

The other impression is recurrent and is, again, eminently a *film* effect. It is a device for symbolising the network of determinism that intertwines the whole action, and is like a view under supernatural X-rays. "A new and penetrating light descends on the spectacle, enduing men and things with a seeming transparency, and exhibiting as one organism the anatomy of life and movement in all humanity." Curious filaments appear, forming a vast web; these are the

fibrils, veins,
Will-tissues, nerves, and pulses of the Cause.

It is in the Fore Scene that the Spirit of the Years first gives this demonstration, and again and again

64

at critical moments through the poem the same weird incandescence brings into view the beating brain of things. Towards the end, in the very middle of the battle of Waterloo, the action is immobilised and, once more, flooded in the unnatural glow. " By the lurid light the faces of every row, square, group and column of men, French and English, wear the expression of that of people in a dream. . . . The strange light passes, and the embattled hosts on the field seem to move independently as usual."

All these are visual effects, conceived by a mind of the strongest originality, and surely they anticipate in the strangest way an art that, when they were imagined, was non-existent. It should be added that sounds play their part, too ; all sorts of sounds : the din of bands, the reverberation of charging hoofs, the music of masquerades, the concussion of guns. Perhaps most memorable are certain drum and trumpet notes that ring out at moments of the action. Hardy was well versed in the routine of the soldierly life (one remembers Sergeant Troy, and *The Trumpet-Major*). In this work he indicates the precise calls he has in mind by bars of music inserted in the text. So, at the Duchess of Richmond's ball, " suddenly there echoes into the ballroom a long-drawn metallic purl of sound, making all the company start." It is the Générale, and the notes of it are recorded. " The loud roll of side-drums is taken up by other drums further and further away, till the hollow noise spreads all over the city." A moment or two later the Assemble sounds and the farewells are taken.

Can one remain unimpressed by the imagination that shaped, by such novel devices,[1] a spectacle of such grandeur?

When we come to the details of the treatment—to what is said, rather than what is seen—we are met by certain difficulties. What, for example, of the poetry? That the conception of the whole work is intrinsically poetical there is no question, but the expression, as such, often gives us pause. The human actors speak, chiefly, in blank verse; it is not, as a rule, very good blank verse, and can be very bad, for Hardy had no distinct talent for this medium. A good deal of prosaic information, besides, had to be brought in, and the poetry, at times, finds this difficult to absorb. Though the news may be very interesting, as that

> There Kellermann's cuirassiers will promptly join you
> To bear the English backward Brussels way.
> I go on towards Fleurus and Ligny now,

it may still lie heavily on the verse. Yet verse, one constantly feels, was the right choice; at its lowest levels it is a reminder of the plane upon which we are moving, does something to preserve the key of the work; and how effective, at its good moments, it can be! In general, no doubt, the mortal dialogue is less impressive than the antiphonal

---

[1] See an interesting discussion in Dallas Bower's *Plan for Cinema* (1936) where a passage from *The Dynasts* is translated into " shooting script." The paragraphs above were written in 1932.

chanting of the Phantom Intelligences. These hymns and choruses, or utterances in " a minor recitative," possess a curious haunting solemnity, a solemnity enhanced by the strangeness of the diction and suggestive of the " monotonic delivery " that Hardy had in mind. " Aerial music " often accompanies them and adds, in our imagination, to the unearthliness of the spectral voices. And then there are the many memorable lyrics, and apart from lyrics, again, a wealth of assorted material that takes us back to what we know and love best in Hardy. Indeed, the vast, ever changing land-scape of *The Dynasts*, for all its awe-inspiring distances, contains many familiar nooks. It is very pleasant, for example, after the dizzy altitudes of the Fore Scene, to find ourselves gently set down on a ridge in Wessex, with old friends all about us. Egdon Heath is where it was and Granfer Cantle not far off. We overhear a conversation, and the style of it is not new to us :

Old Man : Didst ever larn geography ?
Young Man : No. Nor no other corrupt practices.
Old Man : Tcht-tcht ! Well, I'll have patience, and put it to him in another form. Dost know the world is round—eh ? I warrant dostn't !
Young Man : I warrant I do !
Old Man : How d'ye make that out, when th'st never been to school ?
Young Man : I larned it at church, thank God.
Old Man : Church ? What have God A'mighty got to do with profane knowledge ? Beware that you baint blaspheming, Jems Purchess !
Young Man : I say I did, whether or no ! 'Twas the zingers up in gallery that I had it from. They busted

out that strong with " the round world and they that dwell therein," that we common fokes down under could do no less than believe 'em.

Some of the later prose scenes, especially those interspersed among the battle actions, have a quality of comedy, sometimes quaint, sometimes grim, that sends the mind to Shakespeare, as it is sent by so many passages in the novels. In this little interchange, with its bewildering logic, might we not be listening to two philosophers from Falstaff's ragged regiment ?

First Straggler : Well, 'twas a serious place for a man with no priming-horn, and a character to lose, so I judged it best to fall to the rear by lying down. A man can't fight by the regulations without his priming-horn, and I am none of your slovenly anyhow fighters.
Second Straggler : 'Nation, having dropped my flint-pouch, I was the same. If you'd had your priming-horn, and I my flints, mind ye, we should have been there now ? Then, forty-whory, that we are not is the fault o' Government for not supplying new ones from the reserve !

But it seems needless to talk of " influences " : Hardy in such passages feels certain kinds of life as Shakespeare felt them—but feels them again for himself.

Everywhere, indeed, as in the novels, it is the marked individuality of this writer that impresses us ; and it is the same individuality, manifesting itself, in the changed conditions, in similar points of style. Here, for example, is that descriptive precision we know so well, shaping itself often in imagery, sometimes homely, sometimes faintly eccentric, in either case exact. The battle of Vimiero begins " with alternate moves that match each other like those of a chess opening." At Waterloo the allied squares stand " like little red-brick castles, independent of each other." Hardy, it is obvious, had studied the wars so thoroughly that he could see the battles in his mind's eye with the utmost distinctness. Then there is the same exactitude—often of a quasi-scientific kind—in giving the impression of colours and sounds. The evening star hangs " like a jonquil blossom " in the fading west of a cloudless midsummer London sky. The smoke of a bombardment looks " starch-blue." The cannonade before Leipzig becomes, by noon, " a loud droning, uninterrupted and breve-like, as from the pedal of an organ kept continuously down." (These quotations are from the ample " stage-directions " : in other words, from the descriptive portions of the " scenario.") Again, we are continually observing the movements of troops or of fleets from above, from high above, and the vision from there, in the longer perspectives, is just as precise. The transports conveying British soldiers to the Peninsula look like moths " silently skimming this wide liquid plain," or like duck-feathers on a pond, floating on before the wind almost imperceptibly. From our cloudy eminence over Europe we regard the armies of the Allies converging on Brussels : they are " long and sinister black files . . . crawling hitherward in serpentine lines, like slowworms through grass." In the region of the Upper Rhine the dark and grey columns " glide on as if by gravitation, in fluid figures, dictated by the conformation of the country, like water from a burst reservoir ; mostly snake-shaped, but occasionally with batrachian and saurian out-lines." (How characteristic is the quaint puncti-liousness of that last image !)

In such descriptions, and elsewhere, another typical effect is rendered, that of the ironic indiffer-ence of Nature. The last extract proceeds : " In spite of the immensity of this human mechanism on its surface, the winter landscape wears an impassive look, as if nothing were happening." And so at Vimiero, " moans of men and shrieks of horses are heard. Close by the carnage the little Maceira stream continues to trickle unconcernedly to the sea." In front of Godoy's palace at Aranjuez " a mixed multitude of soldiery and populace . . . shout and address each other vehemently. During a lull in their vociferations is heard the peaceful purl of the Tagus over a cascade in the palace grounds " :

> . . . this will go onward the same
> Though Dynasties pass.

Then, too, Hardy (as far as the historical limita-tions of his present theme allow) still follows his principle that fiction should interest by unusualness. There are touches in the detail of the same rich novelty, obtained, not by far-fetched incident, but rather by an amazing manipulation of the simplest elements. Surely no talent of Hardy's is more astonishing than this : I mean his faculty of eliciting the most extraordinary results from the most ordinary materials. One remembers the passage in *The Return of the Native*, in which the youth Charley takes payment for his services by holding Eustacia's hand—what Hardy made of that ! Does not something of the same gift show in this scene ? We are outside the Guildhall, among a crowd watching guests drive up for the Lord Mayor's banquet. " A cheer rises when the equipage of any popular personage arrives at the door." Members of the crowd talk to each other about the war, and their conversation is significant and amusing. But Hardy will not rest content with that. There must be some enlivening stroke, something really novel, something that one does not have the good fortune to experience every day of the week (for there is the core of his philosophy of fiction). Taking, then, the materials just as they are, importing nothing, he invents this : *Second Citizen* is in the middle of shouting " Pitt for ever ! " when he becomes aware, to his amazement, that though *Third Citizen* is making the facial movements appropriate to cheering, no noises at all issue from this particular mouth.

Second Citizen : Why, here's a blade opening and shutting his mouth like the rest, but never a sound does he raise !

Third Citizen [dourly] : I've not too much breath to carry me through my day's work, so I can't afford to waste it in such luxuries as crying Hurrah to aristocrats. If ye was ten yards off y'd think I was shouting as loud as any.

Second Citizen [scandalized] : It's a very mean practice

of ye to husband yourself at such a time, and gape in
dumb-show like a frog in Plaistow Marshes.

Third Citizen : No, sir ; it's economy.

Generally, however, the invention is in a grimmer
key and in such scenes as the well-known " Road
near Astorga," where deserters huddle in a celler,
sharpens sardonically the realities of war. For
Hardy, like certain war novelists of our time, is determined, as far as may be, to show the whole truth.
From him, too, we learn (as it is proper that we
should) not only how a field of battle looks and how
it sounds, but also how it smells ; and not only what
happens in a battle to men, but also what happens
to horses.

Horses ! But, of course, his sympathy extended
far lower down the hierarchy of animal kind.
Hardy was not the sort of man who shares the
feeling of horse or hound, but refuses to enter that
of fox or hare. Still, who would have expected
that in this epic-drama of the wars with Napoleon,
occupied with European conflicts, the clash of
nations and the fall of dynasts, he could find space or
opportunity to express again, as he had so often
expressed it before, his loving tenderness for our
animal kindred, for the small creatures of the field ?
He does find the opportunity ; and no passage in
the work is more typical of his mind, so full of doubts
and high speculations, and, indeed, of deep denials,
and yet so warm in its responses to life. In the
great scenes presenting the crashing tides of Waterloo he spares a thought for the moles, the hedge-
hogs, the larks, and smaller beings still, whose

72

homes were in that field and who were warned of a
" Something to come " from the preparatory movements above :

> The snail draws in at the terrible tread,
> But in vain ; he is crushed by the felloe-rim ;
> The worm asks what can be overhead,
>
> And wriggles deep from a scene so grim,
> And guesses him safe ; for he does not know
> What a foul red flood will be soaking him !
>
> Beaten about by the heel and toe
> Are butterflies, sick of the day's long rheum,
> To die of a worse than the weather-foe.
>
> Trodden and bruised to a miry tomb
> Are ears that have greened but will never be gold,
> And flowers in the bud that will never bloom.

So Nature is crushed and wounded by the human
commotions, while from this novel viewpoint—
underneath—hoofs and heels and felloe-rims loom
in magnified destructiveness. Yet Hardy's mind
is large enough to take in the whole, and the whole
includes glory. The very mention of these combatants, these places, brings a thrill. Hardy felt
the thrill, too. He writes of Marshal Ney, " hero of
heroes," with quickening fervour. And the villages,
the farmhouses—he will pause to dwell on their
very names. The Spirit of the Pities muses of La
Haye Sainte :

> O Farm of sad vicissitudes and strange !
> Farm of the Holy Hedge, yet fool of change !
> Whence lit so sanct a name on thy now violate grange ?

And for a last example of this embracing sympathy,

and especially of the way he responds to the ringing names, I may quote the battle-song of Albuera. It is a lyric of battle, and so, glorious ; but ironic and pitiful at the same time, as only Hardy could make such a poem :

They come, beset by riddling hail ;
They sway like sedges in a gale ;
They fail, and win, and win, and fail. Albuera !

They gain the ground there, yard by yard,
Their brows and hair and lashes charred,
Their blackened teeth set firm and hard.

Their mad assailants rave and reel,
And face, as men who scorn to feel,
The close-lined, three-edged prongs of steel.

Till faintness follows closing-in,
When, faltering headlong down, they spin
Like leaves. But those pay well who win Albuera.

Out of six thousand souls that sware
To hold the mount, or pass elsewhere,
But eighteen hundred muster there.

Pale Colonels, Captains, ranksmen lie,
Facing the earth or facing sky ;—
They strove to live, they stretch to die.

Friends, foemen, mingle ; heap and heap.—
Hide their hacked bones, Earth !—deep, deep, deep,
Where harmless worms caress and creep.

Hide their hacked bones, Earth !—deep, deep, deep,
Where harmless worms caress and creep.
What man can grieve ? What woman weep ?
Better than waking is to sleep ! Albuera !

The night comes on, and darkness covers the battlefield.

THOMAS HARDY AND 'THE DYNASTS'

And what is the meaning of it all ? There seems
a caution here to be kept in mind. Hardy often
insisted that beliefs were one matter ; the impressions of life—" seemings "—conveyed in literature
were another ; and his preface to *The Dynasts* is
especially non-committal. Deeply pondering (as
nearly everything he wrote showed him to be)
" the burthen of the mystery," he was (in his own
words) " no answerer." *The Dynasts* holds no system
of teaching. Still, with this proviso, we are cer
tainly entitled to take it as imaging Hardy's profoundest feelings about life. In the conception of
this poem the doubts and misgivings that so many
a novel had darkly implied are gathered up and,
once and for all, expressed. The thought itself is
simple : it acquires its peculiarly staggering quality
from the imaginative terms into which it is translated. Those Spectres, who chant in their weird
monotones, are like presences from the cold, the
outermost depths of space. But there is a Presence
behind even them which seems to fill the drama.
" Black it stood as Night." We know of it through
the Spirits ; we never see it ; but it is everywhere. It is the Prime Cause, the All ; and the
menace of it lies precisely in its incognisance. It
is not malign, because it is unaware ; it knows
not what it does, and yet all that is done is done
by it :

> Moulding numbly
> As in dream,
Apprehending not how fare the sentient subjects of Its
  scheme.

JAMES, JOYCE, AND OTHERS

One does not forget the names that Hardy invents for this being, the Power behind everything : it is the Immanent Unrecking, the Great Foresightless, the Inadvertent Mind ; viewless, voiceless, hateless, loveless, the dreaming, dark, dumb Thing ; or (and Hardy was the first to give it this ultimate, this most appalling title of all) It : the omnipotent, omnipresent Neuter. This dark Presence of *The Dynasts* is (surely) one of the really tremendous images of modern literature.

It looms over the whole poem, and yet the shadow it casts is not quite absolute. In the midst of the resonant Negative, which sounds through the work, comes a faint, a very faint, Perhaps. Hardy could not claim originality for the idea that the driving force of the universe is unconscious, that the whole of human conduct is, as the spirit of the Ironies puts it, a " mechanised enchantment." But another notion he did think was new. This was the idea of the " unconscious force as gradually becoming conscious," of consciousness " creeping further and further back towards the origin of force." [1] At present, Man is exceptional in a universe unaware of him : " came unmeant " as an accidental upthrust of intelligence ; hence the misery. But in this other fancy lies the slight hope. It enters *The Dynasts* like a little cheering melody, just a few barely audible bars amid the crashing discords. After the

[1] *Cf.* the lines from *Nature's Questioning* :

> Or are we live remains
> Of Godhead dying downwards, brain and eye now gone ?

The reverse process is imagined.

76

death of Nelson, the Chorus of the Years comforts
the depressed Pities :

> Nay, nay, nay ;
> Your hasty judgments stay,
> Until the topmost cyme
> Have crowned the last entablature of Time.
> O heap not blame on that in-brooding Will ;
> O pause, till all things all their days fulfil !

The injunction to the immortal Pities, in prosaic
language, is something like " Wait and see ! " Not
for ever may the Will remain unconscious. And
this (though a subdued note in the poem) is the
note, nevertheless, upon which Hardy ends. There
is a chorus near the finish, chanted by the Spirits of
the Pities, beginning

> To Thee whose eye all Nature owns,
> Who hurlest Dynasts from their thrones,
> And liftest those of low estate,
> We sing, with Her men consecrate !

which is like a hymn ; indeed, it is a hymn of
praise to the Wellwiller, the Kindly Might. The
Pities themselves, Hardy has warned us, are idealists,
" impressionable and inconsistent " ; so their song
carries little authority ; it is, indeed, rather what
they would like to believe than what they do. It
has this effect, nevertheless, that the Spirit of the
Years is charmed to wistfulness by the beauty of
the chant, and though

> Last as first the question rings
> Of the Will's long travailings,

the final word is with the Pities. The concluding

chorus envisages the day when the Will shall gain
a mind, when Its blindness shall break and " a
genial germing purpose " come into Its doings :
when the Power shall know what It does :

> But—a stirring thrills the air
> Like to sounds of joyance there
>> That the rages
>> Of the ages
Shall be cancelled, and deliverance offered from the
darts that were,
Consciousness the Will informing, till It fashion all
things fair !

WILLIAM LISLE BOWLES

TO THE REV. W. L. BOWLES

My heart has thank'd thee, Bowles ! for those soft strains
Whose sadness soothes me, like the murmuring
Of wild-bees in the sunny showers of spring !
For hence not callous to the mourner's pains
Through youth's gay prime and thornless paths I went :
And when the mightier throes of mind began,
And drove me forth, a thought-bewildered man,
Their mild and manliest melancholy lent
A mingled charm, such as the pang consign'd
To slumber, though the big tear it renew'd ;
Bidding a strange mysterious pleasure brood
Over the wavy and tumultuous mind,
As the great spirit erst with plastic sweep
Moved on the darkness of the unform'd deep.

S. T. COLERIDGE.

THESE lines furnish the excuse for the following
sketch. Bowles had his little day, but he was one
of those poets whose chief function it is to be super-
seded : after a short time his poetry ceased to matter.
His claim on our interest is that he once interested
some other people—Coleridge, above all—very much
indeed. He did not interest them all the time. He
lived a long life and wrote steadily through the
greater part of it, and much of what he wrote is,
and always was, without value. Even Coleridge's
enthusiasm dwindled as the years went by. But for

a while the poetry of Bowles, or one volume of it, was not less than an inspiration to Coleridge : a notable fact, after all, and one which seems to make a reasonable commemoration of him proper. His amiability, besides, makes it pleasant to recall him.

Bowles, himself a clergyman, was the son and grandson of clergymen and the eldest of seven children, whose needs taxed the family income, augmented though it was by a " small hereditary property." When he was quite young (he was born in 1762) the family moved from King's Sutton, Northamptonshire, to Uphill in Somerset. Bowles gives recollections of his childhood days. He had an impressionable, imaginative mind, which his parents by their tastes helped to develop. The father was a lover of nature, the mother was devoted to music, and Bowles shared their susceptibilities. He tells how, on that journey to the new parsonage, the sound of pealing bells lured him from the inn and the coach was delayed ; or how, as they travelled by Brockley-Coombe, his father took him by the hand and led him to the vast outlook over the Severn Valley : " the impression of this beautiful scene remains with me still, and I believe, from this circumstance I owe my earliest associations of poetry with picturesque scenery." His own residence at Uphill was not a very long one. The Reverend William Thomas, though a " poor and indigent scholar," had enough, or was determined to have enough, to send his eldest and promising son to a good school. The choice was Winchester. Here Bowles performed satisfactorily and attracted the interest of the remarkable headmaster, an expert in the training of future poets. This was Joseph Warton, whose services Bowles did not forget and to whom later he paid pleasing tribute in verse. He thanks Warton in a general way for inspiring his youthful breast with love of taste, of science and of truth. Warton revealed to him the greatness of ancient and modern poets (he names, of the moderns, Shakespeare, Milton and Ossian), and sharpened his sensitiveness to nature, so that he found every breeze on Itchin's brink melody and the trees waved in fresh beauty for him. And Warton did more still. He " unfolded the shrinking leaves " of Bowles' own fancy, wherefore, his pupil writes in acknowledgment :

to thee are due
Whate'er their summer sweetness.

Bowles went from Winchester to Oxford, and from the one Warton to the other. He was fortunate in his instructors. At Oxford he won a prize for Latin verse and hoped vainly for a fellowship.

It was when he had just left, or was on the point of leaving, Oxford, that an experience of great moment befell him. This was his " first disappointment in early affections." He had fallen in love with a niece of Sir Samuel Romilly. Reasons, chiefly, it would appear, of a financial sort, made the match impracticable, and Bowles set off on travel, gradually extending his range from the wilder parts of North England and Scotland to the Continent. But rambling was not all his solace.

He rhymed as well. It was in the course of these journeyings, undertaken to deaden the hurt of his recent sharp distresses, that he put together, from the same motives, a series of sonnets. Bowles himself speaks of the nature and genesis of these sonnets, and points to their originality. They exhibit occasional reflections suggested spontaneously by the scenes amidst which he wandered during this time of depression : " wherever such scenes appeared to harmonise with his disposition at the moment, the sentiments were involuntarily prompted." The poems, he tells us, were not committed to writing at the time, nor indeed, until quite three years had elapsed. Then, urged partly by monetary needs, he suddenly bethought him, as he was passing through Bath to the banks of the Cherwell, to write down what he could remember of these old creations, but " most elaborately mending the versification from the natural flow of music in which they occurred to him." Having done so, he took them to Mr. Cruttwell, printer, of Bath, and offered them as *Fourteen Sonnets, Written Chiefly on Picturesque Spots During a Journey.* Mr. Cruttwell was not impressed and doubted whether the publication would repay the cost of printing, which would come to about five pounds. However, he was at last prevailed upon to contract for one hundred copies, neither he nor Bowles expecting much to come of it. But the results were surprising. " Half a year afterwards I received a letter from the printer informing me that the hundred copies were all sold, adding that if I had published five hundred copies he had no doubt they would have been sold also." Indeed, the little book went on from edition to edition, until in 1805 it was being reprinted for the ninth time. A last edition, with expansions and variations, Bowles explaining that the pieces " now appear nearly as they were originally composed in my solitary hours," was published in 1837. But the identity of some of the earliest purchasers of his volume was what Bowles chiefly delighted to remember. Robert Southey bought his copy from Mr. Cruttwell's shop in Bath ; Wordsworth propped himself into a niche on London Bridge and, with his brother waiting, obstinately read to the last poem ; and Coleridge inaugurated a Bowles Society at his school, transcribing forty copies of the volume with his own hand.

In the meantime Bowles had been making not altogether successful attempts to establish himself. He hoped to receive assistance from the Archbishop of Canterbury, to whom his grandfather on the maternal side had rendered a service in days gone by. Preferment, however, was not at once forthcoming, and his life, before it settled to its even tenor, was to encounter at least one other distressing passage. He had met a Miss Harriet Wake, daughter of a Prebendary, granddaughter of an Archbishop, and had become very deeply attached to her. But again his hopes were to be annulled. Before, worldly circumstances had interfered ; now, when he had resolved that no considerations of that kind should check him, death intervened. It was a second cruel blow, but it was the last he was called upon to suffer. Some little time later (1797) he married the sister of his former fiancée. Then in 1804, after much waiting for a suitable appointment, he was presented with the living of Bremhill, Archbishop Moore, who had at last come to a sense of his responsibilities, giving him the preferment.

Bremhill was Bowles' haven. For fifty years he lived in this hamlet, much loved by his parishioners and much loving them. His life was sufficiently active. Apart from his clerical duties, which he performed with devotion, he was busily occupied. He engaged himself in county affairs, he acted as magistrate, he studied antiquities, he fought in controversies, he wrote biography, criticism and poetry ; so that, though he rarely went to London, and always returned with pleasure to his country parsonage, his name became familiar in many circles. With his appointment to Bremhill his long life of usefulness was only at its beginning. But it was not from now on an eventful life, and there is little of unexpectedness to record. The most notable excitement of it was furnished, no doubt, by the great Pope controversy. Some remarks included by Bowles in an edition of Pope set in motion a bitter quarrel about the character and talent of that poet. It was a dusty and amusing fight, in which the issues (except to Bowles, and perhaps hardly to him) were never properly clear from beginning to end. His two most formidable opponents were Campbell and Byron ; but Campbell (who really began the dispute) argued on Bowles' side without knowing it, and Byron, though he argued with gusto and brilliance, had only a confused idea of what the theme of the argument precisely was. Bowles was caused much anguish by the persistent misunderstanding, and wrote pamphlet on pamphlet in an endeavour to make his position clear ; but it was quite useless. Everybody believed, and could not be made to disbelieve, that he had denied that Pope was a poet. However, he contrived to plant some of his blows squarely, and was supplied with what was, on the whole, an agreeable preoccupation over a number of years.

He received various clerical appointments. After 1828, as Canon-Residentiary of Salisbury, he was absent from Bremhill for about a quarter of every year. He may have cherished hopes for a while of higher offices. But as for fame, he received his meed, and was well content in the main with his retirement. His physical and mental powers failed before the end. He lived until 1850 when he was eighty-eight years of age, and when but one of his former notable trinity of admirers remained. Wordsworth died almost exactly a fortnight later. Bowles is buried in Salisbury Cathedral, in which he had himself erected more than one monument to worthies of the Church. His wife had died six years before him.

Bowles was fortunate in his rectorship at Bremhill. It was a fair piece of country in which his existence was set ; and apart from that, an extraordinarily interesting and cultured society was available to him. Within walking distance from his house on its hill was the Lansdowne mansion. At this great political rendezvous Bowles was a frequent visitor, and met a succession of people of note. Slightly farther off, but only three hours' walk through Bowood, was the retreat of Tom Moore at Sloperton Grange. Bowles and Moore, with their friends, met constantly, and it is in Tom Moore's Journals that Bowles now lives for us most vividly. Bowles' own home, a double-storied vine-clad dwelling adjoining the church, charmed more than one distinguished guest, both for the loveliness of its prospect and its own quaint picturesqueness. Bowles was proud of his vicarage, and spent a great deal of trouble upon the grounds, which he laid out in an original scheme. S. C. Hall speaks of the surprises which met one at every turn. " It afforded him high gratification to entertain his friends in these grounds and lead them along its labyrinthine paths—here to a sylvan altar dedicated to friendship, there to some temple, grotto or sundial." Indeed this garden of Bowles' obtained considerable fame. Here is his own description, from which the ingenuity of the devices may be gathered : " A winding path leads to a small piece of water, originally a square pond. This walk, as it approaches the water, leads into a darker shade, and descending some steps, placed to give a picturesque appearance to the bank, you enter a kind of cave, with a dripping rill, which falls into the water below, whose bank is broken by thorns and hazels and poplars among darker shrubs. Passing round the water you come to an arched walk of hazels which leads again to the green in front of the house, where, dipping a small slope, the path passes near an old and ivied elm. The walk leads round a plantation of shrubs to the bottom of the lawn, from whence is seen a fountain, between a laurel arch, and through a dark passage a grey sundial appears among beds of flowers, opposite the fountain. The whole of the small green slope is here dotted with beds of flowers ; a step, into some rockwork, leads to a kind of hermit's oratory, with crucifix and stained glass, built to receive the shattered fragments, as their last asylum, of the pillars of Stanley Abbey. The dripping water passes through the rockwork into a large shell, the gift of a valued friend, the author of the *Pleasures of Memory*. Leaving the small oratory, a terrace of flowers leads to a Gothic stone seat at the end, and returning to the flower garden, we wind up a narrow path from the more verdant scene to a small dark path, with fantastic roots shooting from the bank, where a gravestone appears, on which an hour-glass is carved. A root house fronts us, with dark boughs branching over it.—Sit down in that carved old chair. If I cannot welcome some illustrious visitor in such consummate verse as Pope, I may, I hope, with blameless pride, tell you, reader, in this chair have sat some public characters distinguished by far more noble qualities than the ' noble pensive St. John.' I might add that this seat has received, among other visitors, Sir Samuel Romilly, Sir George Beaumont, Sir Humphry Davy, poets as well as philosophers ; Madame de Staël, Dugald Stewart and Christopher North, Esq. ! " Moore treated this garden as something of a joke. "His parsonage at Bremhill is beautifully situated ; but he has a good deal frittered away its beauties with grotto hermitages and Shenstonian inscriptions. When company is coming he cries, ' Here, John, run with the crucifix and missal to the hermitage and set the fountain going ! ' His sheep bells are tuned in thirds and fifths. But he is an excellent fellow notwithstanding."

Indeed Bowles was an excellent fellow. His goodness of heart, his impulsive generosities, his quaint and innocent simplicities, endeared him to his friends, who loved him and laughed at him. Many a story was told of his absentmindedness, as how, having presented Mrs. Moore with a Bible and being requested by her to write her name in it, he did so, inscribing the sacred volume to her very graciously as a gift " from the Author." Several varieties of nervousness afflicted him. Rogers tells how, with his devotion to music, Bowles came to London expressly to attend the last commemoration of Handel. "After going into the Abbey he observed that the door was closed. Immediately he ran to the door-keeper, exclaiming, ' What, am I to be shut up here ? ' and out he went." But this fear was serious and distressing. He had other aversions almost equally inconvenient. As he told Moore, he could never let a tailor measure him, thinking it " horrible " : " The fellow must merely look at his shapes and make the best he can of it. The new coat he then had on was concocted, he told us, in this manner, and from a very hasty glance, evidently." Not less diverting were his slips and errors.

" Bowles, who cannot speak French," runs an entry in the *Journal*, " holding a conversation with the Judge, come from France to study English jurisprudence, and bellowing out to him as if he were deaf—asking him ' Did he know Nancy ? ' pronouncing it in the English way." But he was good company at table. " Bowles very amusing and odd at dinner : his account of his shilling's worth of sailing at Southampton, and then two shillings' worth, and then three, as his courage rose. One of the boatmen who rowed him had been with Clapperton in Africa, and told Bowles of their having one day caught a porpoise, and on opening it, finding a black man, perfect and undissolved, in its belly, the black man having been thrown overboard from some slave-ship. After for some time gravely defending this story against our laughter, he at last explained that it was a shark he meant, not a porpoise." After some of their gatherings, Bowles would feel ashamed of his excessive abandon and would go to Moore for reassurance. " Bowles called, evidently uneasy at the exhibition he made of himself yesterday evening ; but I assured him that nothing could be more delightful, and that such playfulness and *bonhomie* could leave no other impression behind than that of pleasure, which is very nearly the truth." Towards the end of his life his deafness provided additional amusement. " Bowles came after breakfast more odd and ridiculous than ever. His delight at having been visited yesterday by the Prime Minister and Secretary of State, Lord Lansdowne having taken them both to Bremhill. The foolish fellow had left his trumpet at home, so that we could hardly make him hear, or indeed, do anything with him but laugh. Even when he has his trumpet he always keeps it to his ear when he is talking himself, and then takes it down when anyone else begins to speak. To-day he was putting his mouth close to my ear and bellowing as if I were the deaf man, not he. We all pressed him to stay to dinner but in vain ; and one of his excuses was, ' No, not indeed, I cannot ; I must go back to Mrs. Moore.' Rogers very amusing afterwards about the mistake : ' It was plain,' he said, ' where Bowles had been all this time ; taking advantage of Moore's absence '."

Moore's *Journal* contains a delightful series of little glimpses that leave, in their totality, an amusing and perfect picture ; I quote, at random, a few further extracts : " Bowles showed me a part of his library, in which was collected, he told me, all the books illustrative of the divines of the time of Charles I. and the theology of that period. The first book I put my hand on in this sacred corner was a volume of Tom Brown's works, etc. Bowles was amused in the midst of all his gravity by this detection. What with his genius, his blunders, his absences, etc. he is the most delightful of all existing parsons or poets." " Bowles objected to the lines of Burns,

> And yet the light that led astray
> Was light from Heaven !

as profane." " Bowles called : is in a great fidget about his answer to Brougham ; brought me a copy

of it ; showed me a note he had just had in praise
of it, from his friend, the Bishop of London, beginning, ' My dear Bowles '." " Received a letter from
Bowles, with a very pretty poem, written by him at
Sloperton Gate, on his pony insisting upon stopping
with him there." " Bowles called. Asked him to
return to dinner with us, which he did. Is going
pell-mell into controversy again. Roscoe has
exposed a carelessness of his with regard to one of
Pope's letters, which he is going to write a pamphlet
to explain. Mentioned an acquaintance of his, of
the name of Lambert, who took a fancy to go to
Egypt. When he came back someone said to him,
' Well, Lambert, what account of the Pyramids ? '
' The Pyramids ? What are they ? I never heard
of them ! ' Was called, ever after, Pyramid
Lambert." " Dined at Bowles' party. Never saw
Bowles in more amusing plight ; played for us on a
fiddle after dinner a country dance, which forty
years ago he heard on entering a ball-room, to which
he had rode, I don't know how many miles, to meet
a girl he was very fond of, and found her dancing
to this tune when he entered the room. The senti-
ment with which he played the old-fashioned jig
beyond anything diverting." " A visit from Bowles,
who is in a most amusing rage against the bishops,
on account of the transfer into their hand by the
new Church reforms of the preferment and patronage
hitherto vested in the Dean and Chapter. No
Radical could be much more furious on the subject
than this comical Canon in his own odd way. On
driving off from the door, he exclaimed to Mrs.

Moore, ' I say, down with the bishops ! ' " " Bowles sent me, this morning, a Latin epitaph (ancient, I believe) and his own translation of it, with both of which he seems mightily pleased. The original (as well as I can remember) is as follows : ' Hic jacet Lollius juxta viam ut dicant praeterientes, Lolli vale ! ' [1]

> Translation :
> Here Lollius lies, beside the road,
> That they who journey by,
> May look upon his last abode,
> And, ' Farewell, Lollius,' sigh.

This last line is as bad as need be, and so Lord Holland seemed to think as well as myself. I suggested as at least a more natural translation of it :

> And say, ' Friend Loll, goodbye ! '

which Lord Holland improved infinitely by making it :

> And say, ' Toll Loll, goodbye ! ' "

And so we read of their happy days, their glee-parties, their excursions. Now Bowles' head is giddy looking over a cliff ; now he is found in the bar of the White Hart dictating his latest pamphlet on the Sublime and the Beautiful to a waiter, pressed into service as secretary ; now, at an evening gathering he escapes annihilation by a hair's-breadth : " When Butler's *Analogy* was mentioned, Parr said in his usual pompous manner, ' I shall not declare, before the present company, my opinion of that book.' Bowles, who was just then leaving the room,

[1] *Cf.* Dessau, 6746 *Inscriptiones Selectæ.*

muttered, ' Nobody cares what you think of it.'
Parr, overhearing him, roared out, ' What's that
you say, Bowles ? ' and added, as the door shut on
the offender, ' It's lucky that Bowles is gone, for I
should have put him to death '."

But it is time to turn from the picture of this
delightful canon (" Was there ever such a Parson
Adams since the real one ? " asked Moore) to a brief
inspection of the verses that drew once such marvel-
lous acclaim. The praise leaves us a little puzzled
now. The sonnets have charm, but it is a mild
charm, and, to us at least, a commonplace charm.
That, of course, is the point. The charm was not
commonplace just then, and there was something of
real novelty in poems so authentic, if so quiet, in
their strains ; so unaffected, if so unarresting, in
their feeling. Bowles had suffered a grief and by an
unusual faculty had found a simple and natural
voice to sing his sorrows.

The note of the poems is subdued melancholy,
mingled with a certain quiet steadfastness. Nature
was his help in his trouble and the most characteristic
of his pieces utter his gratitude for this refuge. In
rivers he found solace : in the Rhine, with its wild
splendours ; but especially in the humbler loveliness
of native streams, Itchin and Cherwell and Wains-
beck. So he pondered by Tweed and found com-
fort :

O Tweed ! a stranger, that with wandering feet
O'er hill and dale has journeyed many a mile,
(If so his weary thoughts he might beguile)
Delighted turns thy stranger stream to greet.

93　　　　　G 2

The waving branches that romantic bend
  O'er thy tall banks a soothing charm bestow ;
  The murmurs of thy wandering wave below
Seem like the converse of some long-lost friend.
Delightful stream ! though now along thy shore
  When Spring returns in all her wonted pride
The distant pastoral pipe is heard no more,
  Yet here while laverocks sing I could abide
Far from the stormy world's contentious roar,
  To muse upon thy banks at eventide.

So, in typical vein, he recalls a landing at Tyne-
mouth Priory after a tempestuous voyage, and the
serenity of the changed scene :

As slow I climb the cliff's ascending side,
  Much musing on the track of terror past,
  When o'er the dark wave rode the howling blast,
Pleased I look back and view the tranquil tide
That laves the pebbled shore : and now the beam
  Of Evening smiles on the gray battlement,
  And yon forsaken tower that time has rent.
The lifted oar far off with transient gleam
Is touched, and hushed is all the billowy deep.
  Soothed by the scene, thus on tired Nature's breast
  A stillness slowly steals, and kindred rest ;
While sea-sounds lull her, as she sinks to sleep,
Like melodies that mourn upon the lyre,
Waked by the breeze, and, as they mourn, expire.

Impressions like these refreshed the heart of Bowles
after its afflictions ; nor did that other influence fail
of its efficacy, and the music of the bells at Ostend
woke him to a pleasure enhanced by memory :

How sweet the tuneful bells' responsive peal !
  As when, at opening morn, the fragrant breeze
  Breathes on the trembling sense of pale disease,
So piercing to my heart their force I feel.

94

And hark ! with lessening cadence now they fall.
　　And now, along the white and level tide,
　　They fling their melancholy music wide ;
Bidding me many a tender thought recall
Of summer days, and those delightful years
　　When from an ancient tower, in life's fair prime,
　　The mournful magic of their mingling chime
First wak'd my wondering childhood into tears ;
But seeming now, when all those days are o'er
The sounds of joy once heard and heard no more.

Is it strange to hear that these poems did
Coleridge's heart " more good than all the other
books he ever read excepting the Bible " ?　No doubt
it is.　Still, one remembers that he was young when
he read them, and that he was in need just then of
a particular kind of assistance.　How shall we
examine these mysterious transactions of the soul ?
It is enough that the sentimentalism of Bowles was
precisely what, at the moment, the spirit of
Coleridge required for its health.　He tells us of the
burial of his intellect " in the unwholesome quick-
silver mines of metaphysic lore," and of the " genial
influence " that drew him thence to " pluck the
flower and reap the harvest from the cultivated
surface."　There seems something comprehensible
there, and the " genial influence " itself is perhaps
not irrecognisably gone.

There was, however, another interest in these
sonnets : their expression.　Naturalness of feeling
was much ; but here too (and this roused Coleridge
to enthusiasm) a certain naturalness of utterance
had been found as well.　Here was someone who
with an astonishing recovery of independence had

been able to regard nature with clear eyes and to speak of his impressions simply. The two faculties went together. As the vision cleared the fit and natural words came, yet it was just because Bowles through some divine grace had escaped the net of conventional phrase that he could see things so freshly. Once again, of course, we must make a certain imaginative effort if we are to perceive the freshness ourselves. " It is peculiar to original genius to become less and less striking, in proportion to its success in improving the taste and judgment of its contemporaries." This reminder by Coleridge may serve us as our text. The newness of Bowles' diction has long since vanished, but we can still acknowledge a soft charm in the unpretending phrase :

> Soothed by the scene, thus on tired Nature's breast
> A stillness slowly steals, and kindred rest ;
> While sea-sounds lull her, as she sinks to sleep.

" Natural language, neither bookish, nor vulgar, neither redolent of the lamp, nor of the kennel "— we may still agree to that ; nor stiff, nor cold, nor dead-coloured, if dim and with little quality of penetration. We read with a mild and lulled acquiescence, and can understand that the humble sheaf of poems was once found grateful to the poetic sense. Bowles afterwards ventured beyond the circle of such gentle, restful suggestion—his true scope—and in more ambitious attempts his charm was lost. But for this note he had a certain gift, and can generally find fit words for the hush of evening, a peaceful landscape, some soothing solitude. He does not always find them, and has lapses into trite proprieties of diction : " The orient beam illumes the parting oar," " yonder azure track," " the reckless main." Personification, too, is a danger, but as yet his Hopes and Sorrows and Despairs have not become nuisances and are easily ignored. On the whole, the verses of the early volume do " combine natural thoughts with natural diction," are melodious and truthful, and reveal a felt beauty. In his best lines there is a certain not unskilfully wrought identity of sound, rhythm and feeling, though it is usually narrowed to that one manner in which he was really happy. He has strayed by Cherwell

> or when the morn began
> To tinge the distant turret's golden fan
> Or evening glimmered o'er the sighing sedge.

On the slope of the Coomb he has watched

> The poplars sparkle in the passing beam.

And he liked to convey the effect of low sounds in a stilly air,

> When hush'd is the long murmur of the main.

This youthful volume contains Bowles' masterpieces ; he never did anything so well again. But the collected poetry in Gilfillan's edition runs to two volumes of three and a half hundred pages each. It was no difficulty to Bowles to write poetry, and his fluency increased with his age. Only in some shorter pieces, however, like his *Monody on Matlock*, did he recapture a little of the former felicity. Pensively, in these, he takes his station in some delightful vale, or on an eminence commanding a fair prospect, and there " meditates his casual theme," finding content or recreation or at least " some mild improvement on his heart Poured sad, yet pleasing." It is of a little interest, in the more pretentious works, to watch the symptoms of the change in poetry : the fresh delight in nature, and with nature in picturesque and " romantic " moods ; with that, the attraction to the exotic, to strange lands and histories ; in another direction, the rehabilitation of humble life in which new and pathetic subjects for poetry are discovered. But Bowles by now was left behind ; he was no longer a pioneer but a straggler ; and there was nothing that he could do in these spheres that was not already being done far more capably by others. Thus, in *The Spirit of Discovery by Sea* he produces a poem reminiscent of some of Southey's narratives, at least in the remote scene, the geographical lore, the descriptions of heathen rites, and the like. We travel far in the five books of this poem and on no clear system :

> all discoveries jumbled from the Flood,
> Since first the leaky ark reposed in mud,
> By more or less, are sung in every book
> From Captain Noah to Captain Cook.

Byron's summary is very nearly true. Bowles indeed makes a great tale of unity in his introduction, not perceiving that the very compulsion to expound in detail the method by which he has secured it indicates pretty clearly that he has not secured it. Transitions are justified in general by his being " reminded," without his inquiring further whether it is proper or not that he should be reminded. In other respects *The Spirit of Discovery* represents fairly the ambitions he had in mind in most of his long poems, and shows how unfitted he was to pursue them. It is in fact a species of dwarf-epic, full of pseudo-Miltonism. Commencing with appropriate invocation to the shade of Camoens, it passes soon to a resonant catalogue ; in a vision

> He saw in mazy longitude devolved
> The mighty Brahma-Pooter ; to the East
> Thibet and China, and the shining sea
> That sweeps the inlets of Japan, and winds
> Amid the Curile and Aleutian isles.
> Pale to the North, Siberia's snowy scenes
> Are spread ; Jenisca and the freezing Ob
> Appear, and many a forest's shady track
> Far as the Baltic, and the utmost bounds
> Of Scandinavia.

So generally he observes the idiom :

> Let the song
> Reveal, who first went down to the great sea
> In ships.

And we have Miltonic echoes :

> Anon was heard
> The sound as of strange thunder, from the
> mouths
> Of hollow engines.

But the style was quite too high for him and the scope beyond his powers. Even his descriptive passages, which might have been supposed in his line of strength, fail notably. He seems reluctant to commit himself more than can be helped and his exotic scenes amount, after all, only to a pervading " umbrageousness." The poem, too, offers an example of that particularly fatuous sentimentalism to which he succumbed in his later effusions. One of his stagy woodland scenes was the setting for the episode of Anna—the Anna who " performed " with her Robert the kiss that interested Byron. Zarco, one of the scouts of Prince Henry the Navigator, comes upon a tomb (the scene is a glade in Madeira) grey and moss-covered. Inspecting the tomb, he finds the mouldered name, Anna D'Arfet ; and so, neatly, we have the occasion for our episode. Anna would not obey the wishes of her cruel father, wishes that would have consigned his only child and hope to loath'd embraces and a life of tears. Rather, she fled o'er the main with him she loved. He said :

> Haste with me ;
> We shall find out some sylvan nook, and then
> If thou should'st sometimes think upon these hills
> When they are distant far, and drop a tear,
> Yes, I will kiss it from thy cheek and clasp
> Thy angel beauties closer to my breast ;
> And whilst the winds blow o'er us, and the sun
> Sinks beautifully down, and thy soft cheek
> Reclines on mine, I will enfold thee thus,
> And proudly cry, My friend, my love, my wife.

The good Bowles, he feels it all. So they came to Madeira ; but neither ship nor sail appeared to rescue them and they perished : Anna first, then

Robert, stretched beside the tomb he had inscribed
with her name :

> His arm upon the mournful stone
> He dropped ; his eyes, ere yet in death they closed,
> Turned to the name, till he could see no more
> " Anna."

Bowles, however, had not told the story with perfect
lucidity of syntax at every point and Byron was sadly
confused.   In the woods of Madeira, Bowles had
written,

> a kiss
> Stole on the list'ning silence ; n'er till now
> Here heard ; they trembled even as if the power

and so on.   " That is," was Byron's comment, " the
woods of Madeira trembled to a kiss, very much
astonished, as well they might be, at such a pheno-
menon " ; adding, of Robert and Anna : " a pair
of constant lovers, who performed the kiss above
mentioned, that startled the woods of Madeira."
Nor was he at first to be dissuaded from his inter-
pretation.   However, Bowles convinced him of his
error and he amended his note : " Misquoted and
misunderstood by me, but not intentionally.   It was
not the woods, but the people in them, who trembled ; why, heaven knows, unless they were overheard making the prodigious smack."

The *Spirit of Discovery* was Bowles' most pretentious
poem on the larger scale ; in the others no saving
excellences appeared.   *The Missionary* conveys us to
the Andes and regales us with a sentimental story of
a young Indian's fortunes in love.

> I've read the Missionary
> Pretty, very—

Byron wrote ironically to Murray. Some did find it pretty and a second edition was called for. Bowles had published the work anonymously ; now he avowed it and made certain alterations. Very gravely he tells us that he has " availed himself of every sensible objection, the most material of which was the circumstance, that the Indian maid, described in the first book, had not a part assigned to her of sufficient interest in the subsequent events of the poem, and that the character of the Missionary was not sufficiently personal." He points out proudly that, with the single exception of the massacre of Spaniards, all the personages and events of the poem are imaginary. Imaginary they may be, but they are not imagined. Nor, again, is the scenery of much moment. He selected South America, he tells us, because the ground was interesting, new, poetical and picturesque. But his local colour consists of a few marmozets, opossums, cogul-flowers and cocoa-trees. Sometimes, as he points out, he can draw on personal knowledge. " The alpaca is perhaps the most beautiful, gentle and interesting of living animals ; one was to be seen in London in 1812." So we have the tender portrait :

> The tame alpaca stood and licked her hand ;
> She brought him gathered moss and loved to deck
> With flowery twine his tall and stately neck,
> Whilst he with silent gratitude replies,
> And bends to her caress his large blue eyes.

Bowles' remaining flights in the more ambitious kind may be left : *Banwell Hill, The Grave of the Last*

Saxon and others. An occasional line in these long poems strikes the ear, " The sad survivors of a buried world," " Swell to their solemn roar the deepening chords," but, on the whole, the less said about them the better.

It must not be thought, however, that these epics and half-epics kept Bowles fully occupied. There are odes, ballads, elegies, inscriptions, hymns, epitaphs, a dramatic sketch. He commemorates his friends, pays tribute to his favourite music and his favourite pictures, finds lessons in trees and stones. Few noted men died without his honouring them—Byron, Southey, Nelson and many another have their dirges and memorial stanzas. He celebrates private events and public, a visit to his parsonage, a speech of Burke's. Towards the end of his life he composed his *Villagers' Verse Book*, a collection of little pieces for the children whom Mrs. Bowles taught on Sundays on the parsonage green. The object of these poems was " briefly to describe the most obvious images in country life, familiar to every child ; and in the smallest compass to connect every distinct picture with the earliest feelings of humanity and piety, in language which the simplest might understand." Some of them were not ill-adapted to their purpose, and in their gentle simplicity we come near again to the Bowles of an earlier day— the Bowles who had once charmed Coleridge with his " softened tones, to Nature not untrue."

' MACBETH '

If we ask ourselves : what is the distinction of *Macbeth* among Shakespeare's plays ? and, in particular : what quality differentiates it most remarkably from the other great tragedies ? surely we must answer : the extreme rapidity of its *tempo*. Its unusual brevity assists, but does not mainly account for, this effect. *Macbeth* exceeds by a mere two hundred lines or so the shortest of all Shakespeare's plays, *The Comedy of Errors ;* the longest of them, *Antony and Cleopatra*, is nearly twice its length. We are tempted at times (as Professor J. W. Mackail has recently pointed out) to confuse difference of length with difference of rate, and to assume, when we are off our guard, that because a play is long it must be slow, and because it is brief it must be fast. Anyone who visits the films will not need to be told that a very short play—a play far shorter than may ordinarily be seen on the stage—can seem intolerably sluggish in its movement. As for Shakespeare, he was too skilful a dramatist to permit any play, even the longest, to drag. Thus, *Hamlet* is a very long play, but its action, for the most part, is very rapid. And yet, when we compare *Hamlet*—to take what is perhaps the extreme instance—with *Macbeth*, we observe a real difference. The action of *Hamlet* is rapid—for the most part. It is not rapid all the time.

The long soliloquies, though so essential for the meaning, slightly retard, while they are being spoken, the pace of this drama. Again, in such scenes as those which present Hamlet's meeting with the players, his colloquy with the gravediggers, his teasing of Osric, the forward movement of the play has become very slow ; that is not to say that these scenes in themselves are not very interesting. Once more, the lines in which Polonius enunciates his wise counsels involve, momentarily, the virtual suspension of the action : the drama, as it were, pauses for these few seconds while Polonius delivers himself of his accumulated wisdom.

Let us contrast *Macbeth*. At one part of the play the action is noticeably delayed ; this is in the fourth act, where Malcolm and Macduff converse at inordinate length and where the royal cure of the " evil " is described ; here the drama lags a little. But how exceptional, how uncharacteristic this passage is ! For the rest, if we try to imagine scenes in *Macbeth* that might have corresponded to the talk between Hamlet and the players, we feel at once how impossible in this tragedy such excursions would have been. There is a quality of leisure in *Hamlet* that has no place here, for, indeed, no other play of Shakespeare's is so swift, so furious in its movement.

It is interesting to observe how closely this quite extraordinary vehemence in the action of *Macbeth* is matched by the style. The language of the play is full of splendour, but it is a splendour with little of calm in it. The style, of all the varied dramatic styles of Shakespeare, is the tensest, the most excited. The breathless interchanges of question and answer are to a certain degree responsible for this effect :

> Did not you speak?
> > When?
> > > Now.
> > > > As I descended?
> Ay.
> Hark !

The passages of self-communion are in a vein as different as possible from Hamlet's " To be or not to be " ; in general, the soliloquies and the asides are nervous or distraught. So, as Macbeth ponders what the witches have told him, his hair rises at his horrible imaginings ; later, as he consults the sisters for the second time, his heart " throbs " as he prepares to put his question. Again, the occasional violence of phrase (" smoked with bloody execution," " unseam'd him from the nave to the chaps "), the wild magnificence of much of the imagery (" pity . . . striding the blast," " the sightless couriers of the air "), the constant allusion to the portentous, as if the frame of things were indeed becoming disjointed—all these add to our impressions of terror. And even when the pitch of the dialogue is lower, the quietness is often unnatural, the kind of quietness that may mask a rising hysteria. So, after the ghost of Banquo has withdrawn, Macbeth comments :

> > > > the time has been
> That, when the brains were out, the man would die :

the remark suggests feelings barely under command,

likely to burst forth at any moment in shouts of uncontrolled laughter. And there is much the same note, but more terribly subdued, in Lady Macbeth's dreamy reminiscence—the calmness now near that of insanity : " Yet who would have thought the old man to have had so much blood in him ? "

Indeed, the emotional tension of the play is so great, its crises so hectic, that it can only remind one in its course of a fever. Life itself comes to seem like that to Macbeth, and he envies Duncan, sleeping well after all the fitful unrest of existence. Many of the details of the play are like the alarms of nightmare : the voice that cried " Sleep no more ! " to Macbeth ; the restlessness and fright of the slumbering grooms ; the dreams that come to Macbeth and his wife and shake them nightly in terror ; the hallucination of the dagger ; the sleep-walking. And is there not, at the finish, a suggestion of the apathy, the languor, that is left by a long delirium ? Macbeth has plunged on and on, wasting in crime his reserves of energy, sacrificing all hopes and destroying for ever the peace of his spirit. At the end an infinite fatigue descends upon him, the despair of emotional exhaustion :

> Tomorrow, and tomorrow, and tomorrow,
> Creeps in this petty pace from day to day . . .

and

> I 'gin to be aweary of the sun,
> And wish the estate o' the world were now undone.

There is one other agency in the play that

enhances still further this impression as of a fevered nightmare : the lurid colouring. The play is vividly pictorial and seems designed in red and black. The red, needless to say, is the red of blood : the blood into which Macbeth steps so far that it is as tedious to return as to go o'er ; the blood that to his overwrought imagination might incarnadine the ocean ; the blood that " bolters " Banquo, the blood with which Lady Macbeth gilds the faces of the grooms, that is the " filthy witness " on her husband's hands, that, at the last, is not to be cleansed from her own by all the perfumes of Arabia. The play is " laced " with blood.

The black is the darkness ; a darkness not, like that of *King Lear*, reaching to heaven, rent with hurricanoes and split with cataracts. The darkness here, for all the " unruliness " of the elements, is of a different quality—brooding, dense, oppressive.

> Light thickens, and the crow
> Makes wing to the rooky wood ;
> Good things of day begin to droop and drowse,
> Whiles night's black agents to their preys do rouse.

That is the atmosphere of this play. So Lady Macbeth invokes " thick night," palled in " the dunnest smoke of hell," to hide as if by a " blanket " her deed from heaven. This night is " seeling," it " scarfs up the tender eye of pitiful day," and, encroaching upon the hours of light, " strangles the travelling lamp " and " entombs " the face of earth. In such darkness nature itself seems " dead," and it is under the cloak of it—the very stars hiding their fires, that light may not see into the depths of Macbeth's heart—that the crucial scenes of the drama run their course.

The play, indeed, opens in murk—the " fog and filthy air " in which the weird sisters are holding their colloquy—and at once a mysterious harmony is established between these " midnight hags "— creatures of darkness—and the obscure unconfessed impulses in Macbeth's soul. There is even (as has often been observed) a verbal link, an ironic hint of the connection.

> Fair is foul, and foul is fair,

the witches sing as they vanish. Macbeth, entering soon afterwards, innocently echoes the phrase in his own first remark :

> So foul and fair a day I have not seen.

It is as if the pass-word of the evil beings has been secretly whispered in his ear ; and his next utterance, as he challenges the weird women and bids them tell him what they are, is the last in the play that he speaks with a clear and untroubled mind. A moment later they begin their " all hail's " and disturbance has come into his soul.

The processes in this " temptation " of Macbeth (if, for want of a better word, we may still call it that) are shown with wonderful mastery and persuasive power, so that each step affects us as inevitable. We are made to see very clearly, in the first place, that he responds too readily—and with a

strange, unnatural readiness—to the salutations, as
if deep-hidden thoughts, long resident in his mind
and perhaps sternly repressed, have suddenly
sprung to life at these mysterious greetings.

All hail, Macbeth ! that shalt be king hereafter !

It is this address especially that produces the change
in him, a change so striking that Banquo's attention is withdrawn for a moment from the speakers
while he regards with astonishment the altered
demeanour of his friend : and Macbeth has not yet
said a word. Banquo questions him :

Good sir, why do you start, and seem to fear
Things that do sound so fair ?

Banquo's own response is perfectly normal. He is
interested and curious, and a little disappointed
that he himself has not figured in such glorious
predictions, but not in the least disturbed ; to him
the words sound only " fair." They are not fair-
sounding to Macbeth (or if they are, sinister under-
tones accompany them), for they suddenly formulate
—this is the shock he has received—secret and
guilty aspirations within his own breast. So he
stands " rapt," plunged in frowning reverie. A
little later Banquo draws the attention of Ross and
Angus to their " partner," still " rapt," his mind
seething with the conflicting thoughts that the
encounter has provoked ; and later still, it is the
word he uses in his own letter to his wife narrating
the marvel : " Whiles I stood rapt in the wonder
of it." The prophecies of the witches, it is evident,

have set in motion ideas that are stirring his very being.

But, of course, it is the immediate confirmation of the second greeting that makes, so naturally, the profoundest impression on him, for it seems to lend a terrible validity to the utterances of these creatures. Who could have doubted, after this, that they had " more in them than mortal knowledge " ? The witches, as we know, have hailed him with three titles, Glamis, Cawdor, King-to-be. It is fortune-telling on a superlative scale, and we may gauge easily, by the effects this art can exert on our own feelings when we let ourselves be swayed, the state of Macbeth's mind. The first part of the triple salutation is recognised by him as already a truth : he knows he is thane of Glamis. This is like a guarantee of good faith and would have been sufficient, by itself, to win attention. A few moments later, as he is left burning with curiosity concerning the other titles, Ross and Angus come on the scene, and Ross hails him by the second—thane of Cawdor. We can measure the terrible emotion that this greeting sends through him by the exclamation of the level-headed Banquo. A minute or two previously Banquo was calmly interested in the prophecies ; now he shows real amazement :

What, can the devil speak true ?

As for Macbeth, his confused feelings come to us in four successive asides, and we are made to follow with poignant sympathy and suspense the movements of his mind. He struggles between exultation and dread. He can no longer doubt that destiny is shaping events towards a certain end, and the recognition of what the goal is brings an over-mastering thrill :

> Two truths are told,
> As happy prologues to the swelling act
> Of the imperial theme :

" the imperial theme " : his excitement breathes in the glorious phrasing. The second part of the same aside discloses the lurking terror behind the thrill. It is significant that he speaks of the pro-phecies as " supernatural soliciting " : the word " soliciting " is ominous, for the witches have merely announced events, and two have already come to pass without his lifting a finger. If he feels that the third will demand intervention from him-self it can only be because he is permitting his own guilty impulses to come to light, and the sight of them is terrifying to his better soul. It is true that in his next aside he makes to this better part of his nature a formal declaration of the stand he means to take :

> If chance will have me king, why, chance may crown me
> Without my stir.

That is right and admirable, but the words do not carry conviction ; we imagine that their real function is to quieten, momentarily, his con-science ; he is acting to himself. The aside which follows is more genuine, and shows a mind full of trouble :

> Come what come may,
> Time and the hour runs through the roughest day.

But the tone of this is very different and his own position left more dubious. " Come what come may " : but what comes may be through his action ; he is not now committing himself. Our impression is increasingly of his helplessness to resist an awful fascination ; he is being steadily drawn towards some dark deed, attracted by the regal vision that the witches have shown him. Presently a slight obstruction appears to raise itself : Malcolm is appointed Prince of Cumberland : and now, at this threat to what he was beginning to accept as determined by the fates, the strength of his desires is for the first time fully revealed to himself. He admits that they are black and deep, but at the same time consciously wills that to be

Which the eye fears, when it is done, to see.

Yet, though he has already become involved— perhaps beyond escape—the way is still far from simple for Macbeth. How different is his wife ! From the moment that she receives the letter all is clear, no qualm disturbs her ; her only concern is of ways and means. Macbeth has nothing of this single-heartedness. Despite the avowal of his last aside, he arrives at the castle moody and harassed, his face, says Lady Macbeth, a book

where men
May read strange matters.

She takes the future for granted and assumes that their only problem is to plan the when and the how of the murder. But Macbeth is markedly withdrawn, temporises, will not confess that he perceives the sinister double meaning in her words. " Duncan comes here to-night," he announces, and to his wife's pregnant query : " And when goes hence ? " answers tamely : " To-morrow, as he purposes." It is left to her to draw the obvious moral, but he steadily refuses to be enticed into discussion, putting the whole matter off with " We will speak further." It is as if his abhorrence has conquered his ambition, as if the whole grim project has become finally repulsive to him.

We learn much of his nature from this hesitancy. " Fear " is an easy word, and Lady Macbeth, with a practical end in view, finds the taunt effective. His last feeble objection : " If we should fail ? " gives her the chance to overwhelm him with her scorn. But it is clear that the material risks of the enterprise are among the least of his anxieties. Lady Macbeth comes closer to the sources of his trouble when she speaks of his wish to act " holily," a wish, as she interprets it, that springs from mere unmanly timidity. He is, she thinks, too soft,

> too full o' the milk of human kindness
> To catch the nearest way.

And it is true that he has his share of common weaknesses and scruples. He is so far a normal man that he enjoys possessing the " golden opinions " of people and hates the idea of losing them. Nor can he face without a shudder the spiritual isolation that he knows (whatever be the practical issue) will come from violating the code of his race.

The social instincts are strong in him. With all his pride and egoism, and despite the vein of hardness that must always have been in his nature, he has a deep craving to be at one with his fellowman. At the end, much of his despair arises from the thought that he has forfeited for ever the trust and goodwill of his kind :

I have lived long enough : my way of life
Is fall'n into the sear, the yellow leaf,
And that which should accompany old age,
As honour, love, obedience, troops of friends,
I must not look to have ; but, in their stead,
Curses, not loud but deep, mouth-honour, breath
Which the poor heart would fain deny, and dare not.

It is strange to hear the word " love " from the lips of this murderer ; and yet the sanctities of life have never been meaningless to Macbeth, as they were, for example, to the Edmund of *King Lear :* the duty of the host to the guest, of the kinsman to his senior, of the subject to his king. He feels these ties, and the ties of gratitude as well, and has never been able to say—as Richard III could— " I am myself alone."

But we know that a still deeper reluctance is withholding him and that it comes from his own conscience. He confesses to himself that the deed he contemplates is without excuse or justification, that he has no spur to prick the sides of his intent, but only vaulting ambition, that the taking-off is a deep damnation, that the horror of the act will give the virtues of Duncan trumpet-tongued voices, that pity will ride on the air and tears drown the wind. It would seem that none of the implications of what he intends is hidden from him and that he sees clearly that he is about to ruin his soul.

And yet, is it a true lucidity? If it were, his persistence in what he knows to be so vile would be less intelligible. But Macbeth's mind works in a special way. It is not remarkable for its grip or its clarity; it is remarkable for its vivid gleams of intuition and for the emotional excitement with which it can inflame his being. It is not a reflective mind, and indeed from the beginning of the play we notice in him a certain inaptitude for, or impatience of, deliberation. He can never coolly think. Rather, his half-formed purposes writhe in a murky confusion, and he is content that they should, for he is afraid to inspect them:

> Stars, hide your fires;
> Let not light see my black and deep desires:
> The eye wink at the hand . . .

Even the debate with his wife, when certain matters must be acknowledged between them, hardly clarifies for himself what he really desires, so that it is, as it were, with a mind still but half made up that he enters Duncan's chamber. All through these critical moments the artificiality of his mood can be felt. From his flat " We will proceed no further in this business," he has screwed himself, under his wife's tauntings, to the resolve:

> I am settled, and bend up
> Each corporal agent to this terrible feat.

But it is an unnatural, an inflamed resolve. The

vision of the dagger is an indication of the brain
" heat-oppressed," and the whole soliloquy shows
his overwrought state. One aspect of this soliloquy
seems especially interesting. We have heard how a
soldier in a time of approaching crisis—such as the
" zero " moment for an attack—will often observe
in himself a quite unwonted mental activity, as if
all his faculties had suddenly received stimulation.
Is it not rather like that with Macbeth, as he waits ?
His imagination is always quick, we know, but at
such times it acquires an almost preternatural
intensity. During these last seconds before the
deed he becomes vividly aware, not only of the
necessities immediately ahead of him, but of details
that have, in a practical sense, no relevance to the
act he intends. His awareness is indeed for the
time being that of a poet, and he *appreciates* with a
curious exhilaration the artistic rightness of the
rôle he is about to play, for it seems to his heightened
fancy to be required by the hour and the place.
Just as, at a later point in the drama, he feels the
" thickening light "—with the crow making wing
to the rooky wood and good things of day beginning
to droop and drowse—as united in a sinister harmony with the doom he has prepared for Banquo,
so now the silence of the castle, the " curtain'd
sleep " abused by " wicked dreams," the dark, the
witchcraft abroad—all seem waiting for his act, and
the bell that suddenly sounds in the stillness comes
to his imagination as the summons. In this exalted
mood he is nerved for the crime.

But the reaction is fearful. His words as he re-

enters after the murder have lost their excited ring ;
instead, a terrible flatness has come into them. He
looks half stupidly at his blood-stained hands :
" This is a sorry sight " : and perplexes himself
with the problem why he could not say " Amen "
when the two who had been roused from their
sleep cried " God bless us ! " Shakespeare's inven-
tive powers are at their very height all through this
scene and are nowhere more marvellously exhibited
than in these two or three lines. What fatuity it is
for Macbeth to stand—at such a moment—studying
a question like that ! He will not give it up, but
gnaws and gnaws upon it :

> But *wherefore* could not I pronounce Amen ?

It is idiotic and—to his wife—exasperating, yet even
she, for all her impatience, catches a glimmer of
some dreadful import behind this futile harping on
a word, and is momentarily dismayed. His nerve,
too, is now so completely gone that he cannot return
to the room with the daggers ; and disillusionment
is already flooding in :

> Wake Duncan with thy knocking ! I would thou
> couldst !

Between the last two scenes of the second act, and
between that act and the third, some time elapses,
and the change after the interval in both Macbeth
and Lady Macbeth is very marked. The alteration
in Macbeth (now King of Scotland) is chiefly that
he has hardened. How little, after all, his wife
understood of the tremendous strength in her hus-

band, how she miscalculated the forces in his nature that she was unlocking ! Her own vitality is already at the ebb, but he has revived his powers and is fresh in resolution. It is partly that he cannot rest. Thoughts of Banquo and of possible frustration from this quarter fill his mind with " scorpions," and he is determined, now that he is committed beyond any chance of retreat to his evil path, to follow it to whatever finish it may have. Rather than see Banquo (or Banquo's issue) get the better of him,

> come fate into the list,
> And champion me to the utterance !

" To the utterance ! " He will go to the bitter end. The second murder is left half accomplished, for the son escapes, and " rancours " still remain in the vessel of Macbeth's peace. But there is no thought now of relinquishing his objective ; such checks are but a spur to renewed effort. Even his lapse at the banquet he can explain, after his aberration is past, as merely " the *initiate* fear that wants hard use." Lady Macbeth must have felt the irony in such words. He encourages her : " We are yet but young in deed." " Young ! "—to this worn-out woman, already a shadow of her former self. But it is true of him ; he is only now, in his desperation, beginning to draw on his reserves of strength, and they seem inexhaustible.

For by this time a new vein has come into his conduct, that of recklessness. We understand the development easily : it is, in part, that he has nothing further to lose. What in his heart of hearts he always valued most, though he has tried not to acknowledge the truth to himself, was the eternal jewel of his good conscience, and this he has lost for ever. As for further calamities, can anything that may come be worse than the terrible dreams that inflict nightly torment? Better be with the dead than continue in such a life. Besides, he is now so deep in blood that it is as easy to go on as to stand still or to return. Violence, and yet more violence, seems his only course : at the least, it is an outlet for the fever within him, does something to still the terrible restlessness of his spirit. So he inaugurates with the slaughter of Macduff's wife and children his new policy of utter savagery ; each cruel impulse is now to be gratified with instant performance : he has done with " scanning " for ever.

In the last act he has changed still further and signs of the final disintegration are evident. His nerves are now nearly out of control ; we feel, as we watch him irritably receiving the messengers, that his doom is near, that he is indeed (as Malcolm puts it) " ripe for shaking." He is preoccupied with omens, seems more than ever under the dominion of the prophecies : he rests his confidence now in Birnam wood which, in the way of nature, cannot remove to Dunsinane. He obstinately insists that he be clad in his armour, though Seyton assures him " 'tis not needed yet," and we see that his attendants have a difficult time equipping him. He is plainly near the breaking point. The cry of women, the news that his wife is dead, have not the power at the moment to affect him ; he must postpone his grief, for now all but the crucial fight ahead is an irrelevance. Yet even in these frenzied minutes of preparation, with half his mind he can survey in retrospect the course of his life, taking in its meaning and estimating, once and for all, the vanity of the deed by which he had thought to glorify it :

> Out, out, brief candle !
> Life's but a walking shadow, a poor player
> That struts and frets his hour upon the stage
> And then is heard no more : it is a tale
> Told by an idiot, full of sound and fury
> Signifying nothing.

He has really, whatever be the issue of the approaching test, no hope left, but—it is a touch of the tragic greatness in him—he will go to his destruction fighting. It is now that the messenger enters with the news that Birnam wood is on the move ; if the report is true, then all is over ; but the probability only increases his recklessness :

> Blow, wind ! Come, wrack !
> At least we'll die with harness on our back.

With this defiant shout he goes forth to his fate.

The combat with Macduff does a little more than provide the formal conclusion to the story : it illuminates once again, and finally, the essential nature of the man. When Lady Macbeth taunted her husband with cowardice, she took a ready way to cure him of his " infirmity of purpose," but her accusation was unfair. His courage, for all earthly situations, is beyond every question :

> What man dare, I dare :
> Approach thou like the rugged Russian bear,
> The arm'd rhinoceros, or the Hyrcan tiger ;
> Take any shape but that, and my firm nerves
> Shall never tremble.

But, compact of imagination as he is, this man (whose senses would cool at a night-shriek, whose fell of hair would rise at a dismal treatise) cannot maintain his staunchness in face of horrors that seem outside nature : his mind is too excitable and intense, too vivid in its workings, for that kind of courage. So it is that for a moment or two again in this last fight with Macduff (as before when the ghost of Banquo appeared) his valour deserts him. At the beginning of the encounter he is admirable, and, in the compunction he shows, reveals a little (we may imagine) of the soldierly magnanimity of better days. Believing that his antagonist has no chance against him, and feeling an impulse of contrition for what is past, he warns him away :

> Of all men else I have avoided thee :
> But get thee back ; my soul is too much charg'd
> With blood of thine already :

and, as Macduff refuses to retreat, explains that his life is charmed against all of women born. Then he is undeceived—Macduff is the very man he has to fear—and for an instant, as this last assurance gives way and the fiends themselves seem to be jeering at him, his courage ebbs : " I'll not fight with thee," he declares. But the weakness is quickly over. Macduff, calling him coward, draws a picture of the shame of captivity, and these few scornful words, for Macbeth's vivid apprehension, are enough. In a flash he has taken in the vision— of himself " baited with the rabble's curse," " the show and gaze o' the time "—and has turned from the disgraceful sight : better death :

> Though Birnam wood be come to Dunsinane,
> And thou opposed, being of no woman born,
> Yet I will try the last.

So his imagination, which for the moment again played him false, at the end (in a fashion) saves him.

" Lady Macbeth is merely detested," remarked Dr. Johnson. That judgment leaves much unsaid. It is true that her nature must always have been abnormally insensitive, if not callous. Apart from her share in the crime, two incidents show this clearly. The first is her reception of the discovery of the murder. She can hardly have left herself unprepared for this moment, though even if she has, her behaviour is still revealing. She will be obliged to say something when this crisis comes : what shall she say? It is a little problem in acting for her ; she succeeds in part, in part fails. Her first speech is absolutely right. At the ringing of the bell she enters and in a tone a little vexed, a little anxious, somewhat per-emptory (as befits the lady of the castle), demands the reason for the disturbance at so unusual an hour :

> What's the business,
> That such a hideous trumpet calls to parley
> The sleepers of the house ?   Speak, speak !

So far so good.   But her next, and far more important speech, is absolutely wrong.   She is told—or rather she hears—what is the matter, and exclaims :

>   Woe, alas !
>   What, in our house ?

The note is false and immediately draws a gruff retort from Banquo :

>   Too cruel anywhere.

If Lady Macbeth has rehearsed the speech, it means that she has not been able to imagine the feelings that would be natural in such a situation, has not been able to realise that one thinks (or is supposed to think) at such a moment only of the man who is dead.   Thoughts of " our house " come later, not just then.   If the words were spontaneous, they are hardly less tell-tale.

It is noteworthy, again, that she needs to be taught what murder is.   She took back the daggers to the room and looked on the slaughtered Duncan with her own eyes, but that was not enough.   She has to learn from the feelings of other people, has to have the horror reflected to her, as it were, from other minds.   It is not until she stands in the group listening to Macbeth's description of what he found —and he is not sparing in his details—and catches the appalled look on the faces of the guests, that she begins to feel the true awfulness of what has happened.

Still, no one is merely detestable who is endowed with will and courage such as hers : she must always inspire awe. She inspires pity, too, in the end, and this can only be because there lurk in the secret places of her heart some traits of womanliness which not even her inhuman resolution can quite destroy. Thus, it is clear that throughout the first two acts she is subjecting herself to an unnatural strain. It is by exertion of the will that she unsexes herself, makes thick her blood, stops up the access and passage to remorse. Again, her actual part in the crime fell rather short of her initial purpose. Her first exalted words after she had received Macbeth's letter, seemed to picture herself as the agent of the murder :

> Come, thick night,
> And pall thee in the dunnest smoke of hell,
> That my keen knife see not the wound it makes.

Even if we do not press the words in their absolutely literal sense, it is clear that she did for a moment, as she was going about the preparations, have an impulse to finish the dread work with her own hands, but found herself, when it came to the point, unable :

> Had he not resembled
> My father as he slept, I had done't.

It was a weakness in herself that she seems to find curious. It means that she has not, after all, perfectly estimated her strength of will and can be trapped by feelings she did not know she possessed. Significantly, too, she took the precaution of fortifying herself even for her subordinate part in the enterprise :

That which hath made them drunk hath made me bold.

She is firmer in resolution than her husband, and her purposes are more concentrated, but it is clear, even from the early scenes, that she has a mere fraction of his staying power : her endurance is limited, her resources, whether of mind or body, are being unnaturally taxed.

Besides—and this is at once her strength and her weakness—she is comparatively unintelligent. She is efficient and practical, but her range of vision is restricted, and there are realities in life of which she has not yet suspected the existence. Macbeth is full of repressed fear because he foresees, even if in confused glimpses, what lies ahead : the mental agony, the spiritual defeat. Her mind is bent on the immediate issues and she refuses to recognise that there are others which will some day have to be met. To her blood is just blood, a dead man's face merely a face—an object like any other object ; the deed, she affirms, can be cleared with a little water. So later, in the banquet scene, when Macbeth is gazing with fascinated horror at his chair and what he thinks he sees in it. she tries to shake sense into him :

When all's done,
You look but on a stool.

The remark (though in the circumstances we know she could have said nothing else) is exactly symbolical of her attitude. Such commonsense helps her to keep her self-control, as we see in the same scene where it is she who rises to the occasion and does what she can to avert the suspicions of the guests. But she pays the penalty. It is not possible for her to remain for ever blind to the true nature of what they have done, and when at last she does begin to comprehend that a little water will not clear their minds of the deed, whatever it may do to their hands, she finds the hideous revelation too much for her. It is Macbeth's behaviour immediately after the crime that at first seriously takes her aback : she interjects, with a sudden fear in her voice :

These deeds must not be thought
After these ways : so, it will make us mad.

She begins to understand what it may feel like to be a murderer, a murderess : the point had not occurred to her before. At the moment she summons her energies to face the practical task, and persuades herself that her old diagnosis of her husband was correct :

My hands are of your colour ; but I shame
To wear a heart so white.

But in the scene of the discovery, what with physical reaction and the horrifying force of Macbeth's words, she breaks down, and when we see her again, after the coronation, she is a different person. She is old.

It is the very accent of weary disillusionment that we hear in her first utterance :

> Nought's had, all's spent,
> Where our desire is got without content.

From now on she says little. Macbeth never consults her :

> Be innocent of the knowledge, dearest chuck,
> Till thou applaud the deed.

How strange the note of condescension sounds ! Once they argued together as equals. Wading resolutely into the blood, he needs bolder counsels than she would be ready to give : indeed, she seems too tired to think. All her fire has gone, except when, at moments of especial need, she can recover her dominance to help him. But for the most part she is apathetic, and sinks gradually. Two aspects of her nature, however, in this later phase, are brought into relief, and appeal to our admiration as well as to our sympathy. Whatever she may say in her dream life, in her waking she utters no word of reproach or complaint. It is, indeed, a certain greatness in both that in their time of defeat and anguish, we hear no word of recrimination. Macbeth can find a vent for his suffering in feverish activity, but for his wife there is not this means of forgetfulness, and her despair seems the more poignant that it is voiceless. But then, while her strength lasts, she finds opportunities to cherish this husband, through whose mistake and (still more) her own they have come to this pass. It is clear that she was not personally ambitious, at least that it was for his glory that she chiefly strove. Her contempt and castigation were for the ignoble scruples that seemed to be keeping him from the " golden round," his due. And now that her mistake is revealed she makes what reparation is possible by care and concern and the support of her own invincible will when unearthly terrors sap his, a true helpmate, according to her vision, to the end.

It remains to say a word of Banquo, whose story furnishes a subordinate, ironical counterpart to that of Macbeth himself. At the beginning no one could have seemed more secure than he. He is a man (as Macbeth tells us) at once courageous and prudent, a man whose decent and dauntless nature has something of " royalty " in it, a man to be respected, and, if his opposition should be aroused, to be feared. His conduct when we first meet him illustrates, in part, this tribute. The witches disturb him not a whit ; indeed, his bearing was so fearless, his challenge so bold, that Macbeth (when he recalls the scene) says that he " chid the sisters." It is plain, at least, that they produced no slightest feeling of awe in him, and, as for being " solicited " by their words, no trace of such a thought entered his mind.

And yet we may discern in this early scene, if we look closely, the beginning of the end, the scarcely visible speck that will later corrupt his being. He is a little vexed that the sisters have not included him in their predictions : " to me you speak not " ; perhaps vexed is too strong a term : it is a whimsical pretence of jealousy, or less, and is followed by words that have in them a genuinely " royal " ring :

> Speak then to me, who neither beg nor fear
> Your favours nor your hate.

Nevertheless, he has drawn the comparison, however lightly ; a thought has lodged in his mind that was never there before. He continues, through the scene, to treat the matter carelessly, and when Macbeth asks him, as if the possibility really deserved consideration : " Do you not hope your children shall be kings ? " seems to chaff his friend for the undue seriousness with which he is taking the prophecies :

> That, trusted home,
> Might yet enkindle you unto the crown
> Beside the thane of Cawdor.

Yet he confesses in his next words that such events do sometimes have a weightier import :

> But 'tis strange :
> And oftentimes, to win us to our harm,
> The instruments of darkness tell us truths,
> Win us with honest trifles, to betray's
> In deepest consequence.

The history of Banquo (like that of so many an interesting minor character in Shakespeare) has perforce to be given intermittently. When we see him again, at the beginning of the second act, there has been a leap in his progress ; he is much changed, ill at ease and depressed :

> A heavy summons lies like lead upon me,
> And yet I would not sleep :

for sleep itself, because of " cursed thoughts," can yield him no rest. What has happened to the tranquil-minded, self-possessed Banquo of the first act ? We learn presently, when without introduction he says to Macbeth :

> I dreamt last night of the three weird sisters,

adding,

> To you they have show'd some truth.

That last remark is very significant : it is clear that long trains of thought lie behind it. Banquo has been brooding over the strange encounter, speculating on what meaning it may have, wondering (despite his initial disdain and incredulity) how he himself may be involved. The little speck has begun to spread : Banquo's clear mind is darkening.

His reply, when Macbeth proceeds to make the ambiguous overture to him, is as dauntless as ever, for he is not at all the kind of man to be intimidated into adopting a line of policy of which he disapproves ; and in any case, whatever be the part intended for him by destiny, it can hardly require much immediate action : his must necessarily be the waiting game. Still, his choice is not the less definite for that. The murder takes place, and he has so much of the evidence in his hands that in a flash he must have assigned the guilt. He says hardly anything during the scene of the discovery, but before it finishes makes one notable speech:

> In the great hand of God I stand, and thence
> Against the undivulg'd pretence I fight
> Of treasonous malice.

It is a declaration with a threat in it—has the ring indeed of an ultimatum—and we may imagine that while he uttered it his gaze was directed at the thane of Cawdor. Banquo is still fearless, still to be reckoned with.

But the sequel disappoints our expectations. We find that, after all, he took no stand, but was content to drift ; or even, that he assisted the current of events. His duties are knit to his new sovereign " with a most indissoluble tie," and yet he is persuaded that this sovereign is the murderer of Duncan. The reason of his silence he almost avows. So the temptation has proved too much for Banquo. We may guess that if one positive act of evil had been demanded of him he would not have performed it ; but his way was made too easy : he had simply to acquiesce in the evil deeds of another.

The fates of the two men are ironically contrasted. Macbeth risked everything on his great throw, and at his finish is not deprived of a certain sublimity. Banquo, though no coward, has played safely, and receives his ignoble reward :

> *safe* in a ditch he bides,
> With twenty trenched gashes on his head.

ACKNOWLEDGMENT

The essays making this volume were written primarily as lectures—two of them for popular audiences—and have been altered only slightly from the lecture form. The last three have appeared as pamphlets of the Australian English Association, Sydney. I am obliged to the Sydney University Extension Board for permission to reprint the second.

A. J. A. W.